Birdwatching
in Australia
and New Zealand

Birdwatching
in Australia
and New Zealand

Ken Simpson and Zoë Wilson

Principal photographer: Peter Rogers

Bird Observers Club of Australia

Reed New Holland

First published in Australia in 1998 by
Reed New Holland
an imprint of New Holland Publishers (Australia) Pty Ltd
Sydney • London • Cape Town

14 Aquatic Drive, Frenchs Forest, NSW 2086, Australia

24 Nutford Place, London W1H 6DQ, United Kingdom

80 McKenzie Street, Cape Town 8001, South Africa

National Library of Australia Cataloguing-in-Publication Data:
    Simpson, Ken, 1938–
    Birdwatching in Australia and New Zealand

    Bibliography
    Includes index

    ISBN 1 87633 406 1

    1. Bird watching — Australia — Handbooks, manuals, etc. 2. Bird watching —
    New Zealand — Handbooks, manuals, etc.   I.
    Title

    598.072340994

Publishing General Manager: Jane Hazell
Publishers: Clare Coney, Averill Chase
Editors: Sally Moss, Anouska Good
Designer: Andrew Cunningham
Cover Design: Laurence Lemmon-Warde

Reproduction by DNL Resources (Pty) Ltd
Printed and bound in Singapore by Tien Wah Press (Pte) Ltd

Acknowledgements: The authors and publisher gratefully acknowledge the assistance
of Jennifer and Peter Rogers and their son Simon.

Common names used in this book are those approved and published in the checklist
The Taxonomy and Species of Birds of Australia and its Territories, Christidis and Boles,
1994; and in *Field Guide to the Birds of New Zealand*, Heather and Robertson, 1996.

Photographs in prelims:
p ii   Striated Fieldwren (Calamanthus). Port Campbell National Park, western Victoria
p vi   An immature White-faced Heron leans forward and raises its wings ready to fly.
        Jells Park, Melbourne
p viii Juvenile Powerful Owl, with chevron markings, typical of the species, beginning to appear.
        Note forward-looking eyes. Warrandyte, Victoria

About the Bird Observers Club of Australia

The Bird Observers Club of Australia (BOCA), of which this book's authors are proud members, is the major birdwatching organisation in Australia, and welcomes all who care about wild birds and wish to learn more about them.

The club has been at the forefront of a move to encourage native birds back into home gardens, and has provided advice on the encouragement and protection of garden birds for over thirty years.

BOCA has a longstanding commitment to good conservation practice and raises an independent voice on behalf of threatened wild birds and the protection of areas of significant habitat, especially sites listed under Ramsar. Vulnerable bird species currently targeted by special public campaigns are the Glossy Black-Cockatoo, the Beach and Bush Stone-curlews and the White-browed Treecreeper. The protection of ground-nesting species is of particular concern.

BOCA encourages practical, hands-on conservation and has assisted the study and protection of rare species such as Little Tern, Brolga, Plains-wanderer, Red Goshawk, Hooded Plover, Grey-crowned Babbler and Malleefowl. Grants have enabled land holders to fence breeding sites and valuable woodland remnants, develop wetlands and restore degraded bird habitat.

Through its publications (see Further Reading, page 194) the club caters for a full range of birdwatching interests, from those of the novice birdwatcher to those of the professional ornithologist.

Members are offered a wide program of bird walks, camps and extended tours across Australia. They have access to a mail-order library service which offers books, videos, audio cassettes and slides. Field guides, specialist natural history books and birdsong tapes can be purchased from the BOCA national headquarters (see page 195) or by mail order.

Since the club's establishment in 1905 (a time when conservation was regarded as a suspect activity that could be carried out only in private between consenting adults), members have been working for the protection of native birds.

Protecting the natural environment calls for continuing effort that brings few rewards. The same battles have to be fought over and over again. Through BOCA, birdwatchers are offered an armchair ride into the world of conservation and environmental responsibility. Readers are urged to consider coming on board.

BOCA has over twenty branches and affiliated groups in Australia, which can be contacted through its national headquarters. The club is also in contact with a network of other birdwatching clubs and societies, and welcomes readers' enquiries.

Contents

Introduction

A beginners' class run by the Bird Observers Club of Australia (BOCA) was in full swing. Eighteen people were huddled in weak sunlight on a path at Jells Park, on the eastern outskirts of Melbourne. Half of the party had zeroed in on a juvenile Sacred Kingfisher perched low in a feathery wattle. The rest were watching adult and juvenile European Goldfinches in tall dry thistles a little further down the hill.

Around the corner came a low-flying small boy on a brilliantly coloured bicycle. He skidded to a miraculous halt within centimetres of our feet and glowered suspiciously at the group. 'Whadda yous lookin' at?'

Our leader took him in hand for a few minutes, lent him a pair of binoculars, showed him how to use them, explained that we were watching birds, and pointed out the small bright kingfisher. The lad took a little while to focus the binoculars, but eventually he was able to see the bird clearly enough to describe the sea-green head and back, the buff chest and long dark beak.

'Sacred Kingfisher. Yeah.' For a long silent moment he stared at the little bird, then rather reluctantly handed back the binoculars and picked up his bike.

As he shot away along the path he threw his appreciation back over his shoulder: 'That was cool!'

We think birdwatching is pretty cool, too.

This book is written for new birdwatchers. In it we teach you how to look at birds, and give you insight into the links between birds and their natural surroundings. We discuss the effects of light and shade, of daylight and darkness. Not every day is perfect for birdwatching—how will the weather affect what you see? We help you to recognise and understand the daily actions and seasonal movements of wild birds. We lead you on short 'bird walks' in different habitats and for different purposes. Finally, we discuss practical aids to birdwatching, from binoculars to reference books, and teach you how to make the best use of your field guide. We explain the terms that experienced birdwatchers commonly use, and teach you how to describe a bird to an experienced birdwatcher if you need further information from them.

The broad geographical boundary of this book is the whole of Australia, including Norfolk and Lord Howe Islands, and New Zealand with its attendant islands. The Tasman Sea and surrounding coastal seas are included. Collectively, this is a large portion of 'Australasia'.

We do not pretend to know everything about Australian or New Zealand birds. But our collective experience in the field is considerable, our birdwatching knowledge varied and wide, and the advice we received excellent. In the following pages we set out with you on an informal bird walk that we hope will last for the rest of your life. We sincerely hope that you will enjoy the journey.

Ken Simpson and Zoë Wilson
March 1998

PART ONE:

Becoming a birdwatcher

Male Red-capped Robin. Gulpa Forest,
New South Wales

Moulted crest feather of Sulphur-crested Cockatoo.
Wyperfeld National Park, north-west Victoria

CHAPTER ONE

Birdwatching at home

Why do people take up birdwatching? The obvious answer is that it gives them pleasure. Birdwatching is a relaxation, a delight, a distraction and frequently an addiction. We certainly find it so!

Skilled birdwatchers have a very close affinity with wild birds, and can enjoy watching them without the responsibilities of 'ownership' or the restriction of cages. Birdwatching is the observation of free-flying birds in their natural habitat.

The primary skill needed is the ability to remain perfectly still and to watch or listen. All other skills are secondary. This is one recreation in which your level of physical fitness is unimportant, and there are so many ways to pursue the pleasure of birdwatching that impaired hearing or vision are no bars to enjoyment.

If you lead a frenetically busy life, you may feel that you have no time for sitting still and 'doing nothing'. Why not try combining birdwatching with walking the dog, weeding the garden or touring? This turns the faintly disreputable pursuit of 'doing nothing' into a permissible activity. And when you can sit quietly and absorb the sights and sounds of the birds for extended periods of time, you will find it as calming as meditation.

Please give yourself permission to take time out to be alone with birds.

Birdwatching styles

Let's imagine four different birdwatching personalities. If you can identify with one of these, you may be able to imagine how you, as a newly hatched birdwatcher, might enjoy your hobby.

Wanda likes walking. She used to spend her weekends in the bush but, as she acquired family and household responsibilities, she found it hard to get away on her own. Lately, she has made it her daily habit to walk to her local park and back, so most of her birdwatching is done there, or in her garden. She enjoys reading about birds and is happy birdwatching on her own.

Susan is a very sociable person who was introduced to a birdwatching group by her neighbour. She lives alone and enjoys travelling in company with other people to parks and wilderness areas, where she feels safe walking in a group. She likes to have a leader who points out the birds for her. Discussing the birds with other people gives her confidence and increases her enjoyment of her hobby.

Terry is a 'twitcher'. He collects bird records as other people collect antiques. He will travel across the country at an hour's notice to see a reported rare bird. He keeps in touch with other twitchers on the Internet and is very much into computer records and lists: a day list, a year list, a national list, an international list, a life list . . .

Keith is a conservationist. He lives on a few acres on the edge of a large city and works every weekend to restore the original native vegetation and bring the native birds back to the area. Most of his birdwatching is now done on his own property and he is keeping careful records of his plants and the birds that visit them. Once a year, he travels to birdwatch in the most unspoiled parts of the country that he can find.

These people, whom we will meet again later, pursue their interest in different ways, but birdwatching, or an interest in the welfare of birds, is at the core of their recreation. (Keith might argue that his work is too important to be called 'recreation', and we won't argue with him on that score.)

Many books about birdwatching describe it as a hobby that can be pursued alongside other forms of recreation, and of course it can. Birdwatching can enhance your enjoyment of touring, golf, fishing, photography, bushwalking, farming or gardening. It can be secretly enjoyed when ostensibly watching cricket, or delivering packages, or while taking the children to school, and is a guaranteed cure for boredom when travelling long distances. But not many books talk about the *pleasure* that birdwatching provides. Most of the focus is on identification and biology, and not on the rewards. And one of the rewards is companionship.

Even in the centre of large cities, there will be birds somewhere, and for city dwellers the sparrows on the window ledge may be a welcome contact with the natural world. If you live alone, the daily ritual of putting out a few seeds or crumbs for your expectant friends provides companionship and can be a substitute for keeping a household pet.

Children may have their first real contact with birds in public parks, where ducks on lakes are always a drawcard; or on the beach, where seagulls cluster greedily around a child with a sandwich or, unfortunately, around a discarded lunchpack. These are amongst the birds that have learned to use humankind to their advantage, and they are the great adaptors of the bird world. Together with Rock Doves, House Sparrows, Starlings and Common Mynas, they have tended to increase with urbanisation, since they do not need thick woodland to survive.

In a reversal of early trends, many suburban gardens now contain a few native plants. While the destruction of the birds' natural habitat goes on outside the cities, some gardens in established suburbs, especially those close to a well-treed park with native vegetation, may be visited daily by as many as thirty different bird species.

So, set time aside for birdwatching. Even call it 'bird study' if you like. It will be a better description of what you are really doing, because we want you to watch birds out of interest in their activities, not just for identification. We hope you will soon understand how each behaviour fits into the total pattern of a bird's life.

Young birdwatchers. Townsville,
north Queensland

And most of all, we would like you to understand that the lives of birds are in-extricably bound up with the plants and animals (including humans) around them. The world is an ecosystem, in which everything we do affects everything else. Birds do not exist in isolation.

If you become a birdwatcher and begin to understand a little about how vulnerable birds are, you will also become an environmentalist. Sorry, but that's the way it is.

Let's talk about birdwatching in your own garden.

Birdwatching in your garden

Birds in a garden create a sense of companionship. The soft twittering of fairy-wrens or the piping of a robin provides the extra dimension of sight and sound that fulfils the purpose of the plantings. On the other hand, the long-term absence of birds from a garden is usually evidence of serious environmental damage. Conservation, as well as birdwatching, starts in gardens.

What a delight it is to plant a patch of garden especially for birds, wait for the plants to mature and come into bloom and, depending on where you live, record the excit-ing first visit of a Dusky Honeyeater, a Little Wattlebird or a Tui to sip the nectar. You feel proud that a wild creature finds your garden acceptable. There is a sense of suc-cessful communication: 'I provided that natural meal for you and am delighted at your acceptance of it.'

Black Swan and cygnets. Royal Botanic
Gardens, Melbourne

A house is one kind of vantage point—or 'hide'—for birdwatching. Watching birds from inside the house disturbs the birds very little, and may offer the best sightings if your garden is small and most of it is visible through windows. Some people deliberately encourage the birds towards a window by providing a birdbath or a feeding platform. If you can, set up an indoor bird-viewing corner for yourself, with a comfortable chair, and your binoculars and a field guide nearby. Keep a notepad handy (and perhaps a camera) to record bird names and interesting behaviour. Always remember to pencil in the date and time of the observation. One day you may be rewarded by the visit of an unusual bird; but in the meantime you can use this cosy corner to compile a daily birdlist.

In a quiet corner of the garden provide yourself with a seat near a group of bird-attracting plants. We have a bench near a little lake on our property which was intended to serve this purpose. Our problem is that the local Australian Wood Ducks perch on it every day, and rather uncaringly mess it up for routine sitting.

DAILY PLEASURES

We suggest that you make it part of your daily routine to go for a walk, whenever weather permits, and look for birds. Birds wake early. Try to do a little birdwatching every day before breakfast.

When the weather is really too wet, too foggy, too cold or too hot, consider other aspects of birdwatching: collecting books or watching videos about birds, bird stamp collecting, listening to birdsong recordings, going off to attend bird club lectures, or writing up your field notes. But whatever you do, always keep your binoculars handy, just in case . . .

Practising identification on familiar birds every day is the best way to gain speed in focusing your binoculars, for the time when something unusual turns up.

You cannot become familiar overnight with all the birds you may see in your lifetime. The easiest way to learn is to concentrate on a few birds at a time. Whether in your garden or in your local park, never brush off a bird as 'too familiar'. Look, really look, concentrating intensely, at every bird you see, until you are sure you can confidently describe its general shape, size, eye colour, beak shape, leg colour and the colours of its plumage from every conceivable angle.

'But once I've identified a Common Blackbird I don't need to do all that every time!'

Yes, you do. For two reasons. First: if you have been confidently identifying a black bird with a yellow beak as a male blackbird, are you sure you know what a female blackbird looks like? Or a juvenile when it is not long out of the nest and is beautifully streaked and speckled a rich brown? Second: when you know blackbirds so well that you can identify them without fail from the flash of half an eye and a beak in the centre of a bush, or from a glimpse of a shadow flying away into the distance with a sharp chattering alarm call, *then* you will know when the bird in front of you is absolutely, definitely, unmistakably *not* a blackbird. You will become suddenly alert. 'Hey—what was *that*?'

It is this ability to recognise the unusual instantly, *because you know your common birds so well*, that lifts you above the 'ordinary crowd' of well-meaning but bird-ignorant citizens. You have acquired a skill. You are gaining confidence.

An expert birdwatcher is as familiar with the plumage of four to six hundred species as you will become with your first thirty-six. In Chapter Three, on bird families, we provide a few shortcuts for you to gain some ground on them.

Feeding birds

There is some debate over the matter of feeding birds in the garden. Some people see no harm in it, others regard it as an immoral act. Like everything else, the best approach is one of moderation. It is when feeding is taken to extremes that things can go badly wrong.

What do we mean by extremes?

If you enjoy watching the birds eat the supplementary food you provide, you must take responsibility for the outcome. Studies by the Bird Observers Club of Australia have confirmed that supplementary feeding increases the *numbers* of any single species in the garden, but does not necessarily increase the *variety* of different birds you will see. Only a garden planted especially for birds will do that.

One of the buzz words in environmental circles at the moment is biodiversity, which (roughly translated) means that it is better to preserve a variety of different plants and animals in an area than to allow a single species to dominate. Biodiversity is the preservation of a large and varied pool of genetic material. There are many shades of meaning to biodiversity, but in the context of bird conservation it supports the preservation of rare or vulnerable species. In your bird garden, biodiversity means a balanced mixture of plants supporting a variety of other creatures. Planting a mixture of trees, shrubs and ground covers is more beneficial to birds than a bare lawn with one specimen tree and a feeding tray. Suburbs newly cleared for housing are most in need of indigenous shrubs and trees to replace those recently felled by developers.

There is such a choice of nectar-bearing shrubs available that the feeding of artificial nectar, in particular, can hardly be justified. Apart from the dangers of attracting honeybees and wasps, and the care that must be taken to make sure the mixture does not ferment in hot weather, a nectar-feeder may be 'adopted' by aggressive honey-eaters such as wattlebirds, which drink too much of the artificial supply for their own health's sake, and also drive the smaller honeyeaters out of your garden.

Seed supply has drawbacks, too. If you provide small seed you will encourage the introduced sparrows and turtle-doves. In the heart of a city this may not upset the natural balance, but if you live outside the major cities there are real dangers in encouraging introduced species into your area.

Pacific Black Duck. Queen Victoria
Gardens, Melbourne

Yellow-faced Honeyeater feeding from grevillea
flowers in a home garden.

Never provide so much food that the birds become dependent on it. Food from supermarkets is always second best for birds. If you ever begin to think how nice it is that the birds depend on you, remember that you are not their mother—start weaning them immediately. If, for any reason, you are suddenly unable to feed them for a few days, some may die, and not only from starvation.

By providing so much food you have created an artificial 'territory' in your garden. If the food supply suddenly disappears, the birds will slowly disperse into the surrounding territories of other birds. Until the population finds its natural level again, many birds in the area will be under stress, and some may die in territorial fights.

Wherever you live, feed only as much as will be eaten within half an hour and every now and again deliberately miss a day. It is cruel to feed so much, and so regularly, that the birds become dependent on you for food. We're talking about the pleasures of watching wild birds, not encouraging overweight suburban freeloaders.

Birds fed too much and too often will eventually:

- grow too fat
- suffer disease because they are eating an unnatural diet
- become a nuisance to the neighbours through noise, excrement and casual vandalism
- lose some of their drive to find food for themselves.

Place birdbaths and feeding stations near a dense, perhaps prickly bush where the birds can quickly hide from predators such as cats and hawks. Of course, if there are cats in your neighbourhood you will have to be doubly careful about the placement of these attractions. If your cat, or the neighbours' cat, has ever, *ever* been seen to catch a bird, swinging them from a branch (the birdbaths, not the cats) may be the only answer. Wandering cats soon learn bird-feeding times and will treat your garden as a regular meal stop. Hosing them with water can be very effective. Some municipalities have curfews for cats during the hours of darkness, but dawn and dusk provide excellent hunting as well, so you should do everything within the bounds of reason (no cruelty, please) to exclude cats from your garden.

Predators such as Collared Sparrowhawks are just as smart at learning that 'the house on the corner' entices small birds into the back garden at regular times. A Brown Goshawk may dive on a rosella or turtle-dove eating seed on the lawn, sending all the other feeding birds up with a rush of wings. Kookaburras and currawongs will happily accept food from you, but may also snatch small birds to feed their nestlings. Depending on your sympathies you may feel that all this is either unfair or just the balance of nature. Your defence is to provide as much shelter for small birds as you can.

Water in the garden

The one thing we *would* encourage you to provide for the birds in your garden is water. Many of us gain much pleasure from setting up a birdbath and watching 'our' birds fly in daily for a drink and a bathe. But don't provide a source of water in your garden unless you keep it permanently filled. Birds will come to rely on the water, and its sudden absence will be distressing, particularly in hot weather. Check the water twice daily in summer. Birds drink and bathe in winter as well, so don't let water stay frozen for long. In deeper water, place an object such as a rock or sloping branch to enable birds to climb to safety if the depth takes them by surprise.

Birdbaths should have:

- clean and shallow water
- non-slip surfaces
- thick cover nearby for safety
- an overhanging perch
- protection from cats
- shade from midday and afternoon sun, to keep the water and the birds cool.

Ideally, you should provide several different water sources at different heights, above-ground and at ground level. Some parrots enjoy clambering down vines or wires to a birdbath. Wrens, thornbills, honeyeaters and robins will take daily baths in shallow bowls. Set them low beside sheltering bushes that provide safe access to the water. Long, open stretches of water are used by kookaburras, Red Wattlebirds and swallows for dash-bathing or drinking. Pigeons, cockatoos and finches drink happily at ground level at natural pools or from dishes.

A source of water (not just at home but in the bush, too) offers marvellous opportunities for birdwatching and photography. Place a seat within easy viewing distance of a birdbath and make it a habit to sit there for half an hour at dusk. Even in winter, it is surprising how many small birds drink or bathe before going to their night-time roost. If you live in a garden large enough to have a pond or a wetland, consider creating a natural screen that will act as a permanent hide. Waterbirds are frequently shy.

But remember, please remember—once you have placed water in the garden, keep it replenished all year. Small birds, particularly, will rely on finding water quickly, and if you fail them in hot weather the consequences may be fatal.

Home hazards for birds

Some bird behaviour denotes distress, and you need to be able to recognise this and know what to do about it.

Many bird problems can be solved by trying to understand the bird's behaviour from the *bird's* point of view. At BOCA we were quite distressed to receive a letter from a self-confessed 'birdlover' who took much pleasure in a Song Thrush that tapped constantly at her window for several weeks. She interpreted the tapping as 'friendly conversation' as it fluttered and panted with beak open on the other side of the glass. She missed it when it left, and hoped it would return to 'talk' to her again. With a better understanding of bird behaviour, she would have taken steps to alleviate the bird's distress because, far from making friendly overtures, it was waging war on the 'rival' it saw reflected in her window. This is a very common behaviour of many birds (not always males), including fairy-wrens and scrubwrens, most robins, magpie-larks and blackbirds. Kookaburras have been known to break windows by diving at the rivals they see reflected there; fortunately, they come to little harm themselves because they are accustomed to diving to the ground for food.

If this sort of behaviour happens at your house, the solution is to break up the reflection in some way. Go outside and place yourself in the same position as the bird. It may be quite a small patch of reflective surface that needs blocking, either by smearing it with a powdery kitchen cleanser or taping white paper over the area. If

that doesn't work, a thin curtain of material such as black fruit netting hung down from the eaves of the house will provide a barrier between bird and glass and save both of you from complete exhaustion.

Some birds try to fly through a patch of scenery or sky that they see reflected in a window, and break their necks in the process. Birds may 'fly through' a glassed-in corner of the house. Birds of prey, doves and pigeons, rosellas, kookaburras, small

A Grey-crowned Babbler prepares to fight its own reflection in a car side mirror.

The Grey Fantail is a conspicuous forest songbird, its aerial behaviour
often distracting observers' attention from more serious birdwatching.
Bool Lagoon, South Australia

cuckoos and small honeyeaters seem to be at greatest risk. Again, breaking up the
reflection is the answer, but it needs to be more permanent. Some people use black
hawk shapes, on the principle that birds will avoid a predator, but anything that, from
the bird's point of view, hangs in the patch of sky will be effective. You can use window decals, hanging leadlights, pot-plants, wind chimes, or a bead curtain. Just
remember to approach the problem from outside the window. A dark curtain drawn
across the inside will still allow exterior reflections on the glass.

In the breeding season you may need to pull small bags over the wing-mirrors and
lean boards against the hub caps of your parked car to stem the aggression of small
birds.

Are all bird problems fixable? Not when relations with your neighbour are
strained to breaking point because the shrieking of lorikeets at *his* feed table is
driving you crazy; or *her* cat spends all day stalking the finches in your garden; or
cockatoos, bored with waiting for your neighbours to fill *their* seed-bowl, are chewing
your window-frames into fragments.

One behaviour that particularly troubles those who like birds is the occasional
attack on humans. Apparently Canberra is not only Australia's national capital, but
also its capital for Australian Magpie attacks. There is some evidence that the magpies are most likely to dive-bomb small boys and that this is a learned response. One
solution is to wear a hat with large eyes painted at the back, on the principle that the
bird will not attack while it is being 'watched'.

A BIRD WALK IN OUR GARDEN

If you are interested in birds, you are probably already aware of some of the birds that frequently visit your garden. You might already be in the habit of taking mental note of the birds around you when camping, bushwalking, or strolling in your local park. But perhaps you see only the obvious ones, the noisy ones, the 'pushy' ones. When we talk of a 'bird walk', however, we imply a deeper concentration on birds and their activities.

Join us on a bird walk around our garden.

We live in south-east Australia, in a long shallow valley between two thickly forested low ranges about sixty kilometres due east of Melbourne, Victoria. Half a kilometre away are the lower slopes of Mount Ben Cairn to our east, and the Mount Toole-be-wong Range to our west.

One and a half hectares in size, this is a garden for birds, with low ground cover, a middle storey of bird-attracting shrubs, and many tall old trees, mostly the original forest remnants. The season is spring, and the time eleven o'clock in the morning. The sun has just come out again after a light shower of rain.

As soon as we step out of the house we hear the thin twittering of small birds in the bank of low fish-ferns near the front door. Occasionally the fronds tremble as the birds pass through, but at first there is nothing else to see.

Then, one by one and flying low, they cross the open lawn in front of us. Their long tails seem to drag them towards the ground so that they progress in dips and waves just high enough to clear the grass. Out of the thick patch of hebe and fine-leafed grevillea where they land comes a repetitive tinkling song and then (the final confirmation) the male of the family pops up at the top of a bush and sings in full view. Long dark blue tail held vertically, bright blue and black head and back, it is unmistakably a male Superb Fairy-wren, and the others in the group are his brown wife and children.

A black bird hops, both feet together, along the edge of the lawn, pausing frequently to listen for movement beneath its feet. It catches sight of us and takes flight, chinking its alarm call as it flies. Its bright yellow beak and eye ring tell us that it is a mature male Common Blackbird.

On the boundary of the lawn is a pedestal birdbath under the protection and shade of a broad-leafed sycamore. A tinkling call, similar to the fairy-wrens' but with a stronger, rising inflection, draws our attention to a small greyish bird that repeatedly opens and shuts its long dark grey and white tail as it twists and turns on a small branch. Every so often it dives in pursuit of an insect, pirouetting gracefully in the air just beyond the outer branches of the tree. Sometimes we get a quick glimpse of a soft tan chest and a dark face with a white eyebrow. This is a Grey Fantail, one of the most widespread flycatchers in Australasia.

Bird calls are coming to us from outside the garden. We can hear the familiar 'kook-kook' of alarm from the Laughing Kookaburras that breed in the old white gum across the road. In a few weeks they will park their youngsters in our trees and catch small skinks for them in the mulch of our garden beds. Our lizard population takes a real pasting in spring.

Raucous screams waft down the valley as three Sulphur-crested Cockatoos fly high from ridge to ridge. On some days they swoop down to investigate our tallest trees, and instantly the kookaburras gather to defend their territory. The ensuing shrieking and occasional aerial battle may last for twenty minutes. But today, watched warily by the kookaburra family, the cockatoos fly past, their rounded wings appearing snow-white against the dark blue-green hills.

So far we have hardly needed our binoculars. We turn to our right and walk towards a stand of stringybarks and swamp gums. High in the top branches a bird sounds a single sweet piercing note. It is several moments before we trace the call to a sturdy grey shape, somewhat similar in size to a Common Blackbird.

Patience is needed here. The bird reveals itself only briefly as it makes short flights from one thick branch to another, then disappears amongst the outer leaves. Fussing around it is another Grey Fantail, making it hard for us to concentrate on our target. Fantails are often a distraction in our garden.

At last, a good view of the bird as it cocks its head and watches something in the leaves above. Thick head and neck, short strong beak; prominent soft dark eye, a light grey bird with mid-brown on the back and wings. It could be one of the female whistlers, but its larger size indicates that it is a Grey Shrike-thrush.

Then, as a quick bonus, a soft chirring call heralds the arrival of a much longer pale grey bird that lands in the top of the same tree. Over its eyes it wears a black mask that extends down to its chin, throat and upper breast and contrasts strongly with its lovely pale grey plumage. Alighting, it shuffles its wings, placing each wing into position several times as if folding them carefully away for storage. This is the very common Black-faced Cuckoo-shrike, a warm-season migrant to our garden, although a few birds are present all year round in the Melbourne region.

Down a narrow path of shredded bark below the gums we pass a patch of grevilleas and a low terracotta bird bowl. No one is using the water at this time of day, but two Eastern Spinebills are competing for the territory around the grevilleas. They chase each other to and fro across our path with a 'prrrrp' of wings and the flash of white on outer tail feathers that is characteristic of these elegant birds. Occasionally one of them perches for long enough to announce ownership of the territory with a long series of high piping calls. We refill the bird bowl with clean water and press on.

Further down the same path another spinebill feeds from a bottlebrush. As it leans upwards to insert its long, curved-needle beak into a crimson flower, we have time to appreciate the strong blue-grey of its back and its rich chestnut and white breast, banded on either side by a curving black line.

This corner of the garden contains many tall stringybarks and as we stand admiring the spinebill, small twigs and seed-cases begin falling on our heads. We step backwards and cautiously peer up into the treetops. You must be wary of looking up under feeding birds: 'things' can fall in your eyes.

Above us, a metre apart, a pair of adult Crimson Rosellas are quietly feeding, but it takes a moment to find them, as their bright crimson and blue feathers look like shadows against the green leaves. Seeing them on the ground it is hard to understand how such brilliant, contrasting colours can provide such camouflage in the trees, but they do.

We turn slowly back towards the house and freeze on the spot as we catch sight of a small grey-backed bird which flicks up from the lawn to perch on a wattle only metres away. One foot above the other, leaning slightly outwards as it peers downward, it seems to hang sideways on the vertical trunk, so still that it almost disappears against the dark grey bark. It is impossible to tell for certain whether this is a rare bird or a common one, although we already know from its stance on the trunk that it is going to be a robin. We stand absolutely still and quiet, and wait.

The bird drops to the ground, pauses for a second, then flies back to its perch carrying a thin earthworm. This time it faces us, and we see the lemon breast and blue-grey head of an Eastern Yellow Robin. Its large dark eye has the same soft look as the Shrike-thrush's, and both species are quiet, companionable residents of our garden. We can walk on slowly now as long as we make no sudden movements to scare the robin away.

The bushes ahead are full of small birds which have been moving steadily around the garden towards us. A travelling flock like this appears at about eleven most sunny mornings (on windy, wet or cold days, the passage of the birds is less obvious). Locally travelling, mixed feeding flocks such as this are a feature of the bush in Australia, more particularly in the late summer to early spring.

The birds are constantly on the move, dashing around the bushes, flying through the trees, never really pausing long enough to allow us to focus our binoculars, which makes identification difficult, especially as most of them are tiny brown and olive birds and the group includes two more Grey Fantails flitting about at eye level.

Another problem is that we have just turned towards the bright morning sun. Glare makes identification harder. We will have to use sound as well as sight to sort them out.

We move into a patch of shade to keep the sun out of our eyes, and listen intently. Almost at ground level in a wattle we hear the rich warble of a Brown Thornbill, but the bird we first catch sight of amongst the outer branches is olive green with greyish flanks and white eye rims. Easy—a Silvereye. But why only one? Usually they go through in small groups.

In the eucalypt above it we can hear the 'zzt-zzt' of Striated Thornbills mixed with other sharp insect-like calls. We suspect that White-naped Honeyeaters are up there, too, as we have often seen them in these mixed groups and we can hear the faint crackle of bark as they search for insects. But both species are too high in the tree for us to be sure: the tiny thornbills oval-bodied with short tails, frantically busy; the honeyeaters appearing only as slender black silhouettes against the sky.

Suddenly a Brown Thornbill gives a strong buzzing alarm call from the outer branches of the wattle. We quickly bring up our binoculars to check its dark brown eye and plain brown forehead and, as we do, the whole mixed flock disappears and there is sudden silence. A Pied Currawong has landed in a tree nearby.

As it sits sideways on a bare branch we can see the white rump that distinguishes it from the Grey Currawong. But only for a moment. With a screech of anger and a sharp swish, swish, swish of wings, our resident pair of Australian Magpies attacks the intruder, and as they drive it out of the garden we can see the white patches in the currawong's wings and the white tip of its tail. The magpies retire to their nest tree on the hill and carol their 'victory'.

The small birds remain silent. It will take several minutes before they have the confidence to come out of hiding. We've been out for forty minutes. Our morning bird walk is over.

This bird walk has introduced you to many of the birdwatching skills that will be discussed in more detail in later chapters of this book. Habitat, territorial behaviour, identification through sight and sound . . . it is not necessary to travel great distances to derive great pleasure from the use of your birdwatching techniques.

Before you begin the next chapter, we need to introduce a few terms—*family, genus, species* and *subspecies*—which you will meet quite frequently in your reading.

FAMILY, GENUS, SPECIES, SUBSPECIES

Let's look at an example: the Cormorant family, the Phalacrocoracidae.

Within each family of birds there is at least one group of genera (plural of genus) further divided into individual species. The genus is a subjective grouping which implies genetic similarity.

Broadly, a species means 'a kind of'. Note that the word species is both singular and plural (there is no such thing as a 'specie').

Each different kind of bird has a generic name (cormorants are all named *Phalacrocorax* at present) and a specific name, to differentiate it from all others of the same genus. The Pied Cormorant is *Phalacrocorax varius*. It is always necessary to use both names when you name a species, as it is the second name that gives the full identity—just like a given name and a surname, but in reverse order.

It is sometimes necessary to further divide a species. Minor permanent differences within a species, and/or widely separated, sometimes geographically cut-off, populations of a species are given a third distinguishing name. It is called a subspecies (or a 'race'). In the Pied Cormorant, the Australian population was judged to be different from the first-named New Zealand population and it was therefore given the subspecific (race) name *Phalacrocorax varius hypoleucos*. The New Zealand birds are the nominate (first-named) subspecies *Phalacrocorax varius varius*.

'Form' or 'morph' (previously 'phase', although this word has lost popularity) is a term used to describe permanent colour differences between individuals in bird populations of the same species—for example, Stewart Island Shag, Grey Goshawk.

'Cline' refers to gradual changes across a region, in such a way that a sample from either end of the region may *appear* different enough to be viewed as a possible subspecies.

PART TWO:

Looking at birds

Tall Open Forest (also called southern temperate wet sclerophyll forest). Tree ferns (*Dicksonia*), Antarctic Beech (*Nothofagus*) at left and Blackwood Wattles (*Acacia*) at right, in a beautiful gully. Tara-Bulga National Park, eastern Victoria

A flock of Australian Pelicans preparing to roost on an island. Massive bills and flexible gular pouches are clearly visible. There is a Great Egret in the background. Menindee Lakes, western New South Wales

CHAPTER TWO

Habitats

Bird species can be variously classified by family (Halcyonidae, the Kingfishers), or perhaps by physical features (those with red eyes, those with black chins, those with crests), by place of origin (endemic, introduced), by behaviour (sedentary, nomadic, migratory) or according to habitat (birds of the dry inland, birds of creeks and rivers, birds of the seashore).

We will be discussing all these concepts in separate chapters, but let's begin with habitat, because it is by far the most important. A bird's habitat is where it lives: a place where it can find water, food, shelter and the conditions that enable it to breed successfully. Breeding is usually considered successful if the young are fledged and leave the nest, but real success is when the young reach adulthood and start their own breeding cycle. Only then can the survival of a species be assured.

There are about twenty-three major bird habitats in Australia and some of these are very obviously shared with New Zealand. A few are better developed in one country than the other, such as the inland deserts of Australia, or the Alpine Region of New Zealand. All habitats have been modified by humans to some degree. The need for habitat retention and rehabilitation is now urgent throughout the world.

MAJOR HABITATS

AUSTRALIA
Closed forest, Open forest, Woodland, Heath, Low shrubland
Gibber plains, Closed grassland, Tussock grassland, Hummock grassland

NEW ZEALAND
Exotic forest, Southern beech forest, Lowland rainforest, Lowland forest & scrub, Sub-Antarctic

COMMON TO BOTH COUNTRIES
Alpine and sub-alpine vegetation, Cliffs and exposed rock faces, Inland waters and coastal estuaries, Salt marshes, Mangroves, Marine habitats (coastal seas & ocean), Coastal dunes, Islands, Caves, Agricultural and pastoral lands, Plantations (usually exotic forest trees; can be native monocultures), Urbanised and industrial land

Types of habitat

Habitats may be classified in various ways: by climate (tropical, coastal), by the plants that dominate it (beech forest, tussock grassland, alpine heath), or by the geological landform (cliffs, desert sand dunes, coral cays).

Birdwatchers often classify habitats another way: by the birds that live in them. They will point to a stretch of country and say, 'That's good lyrebird habitat.' They are probably speaking from their own experience (that is, they have frequently seen or heard lyrebirds there) and implying that the chances of sighting those species are high. Once you are accustomed to looking for lyrebirds or robins in certain habitats, you quickly recognise the same generalised landforms or vegetation when you see them in another place, and can say confidently, 'This is where I would expect to find robins.' This is a case of experience leading to some deductive birdwatching.

Birdwatching tour guides and group leaders plan most trips on the basis of habitat. They may reason, 'If we go to the rainforest up there we ought to see twenty-two bird species in a day, but if we go to the wetland, near the beach at the estuary of the So-and-So River, we could see seventy-two bird species in the same time.' If their goal is to see three *rare* species in a day, it may take all day to find them, even if the birds are somewhat localised. Generally speaking, birdwatchers travel to their selected habitat with several possible goals, which vary with season, weather or time available.

Classifying habitats according to vegetation types is generally the most useful for birdwatching, although obviously if you talk of rainforest birds or dry woodland birds, climate as well as vegetation is involved.

Habitats and birdwatching

Which are the richest habitats for birdwatching?

It depends what you are looking for. If your heart is set on seeing thousands of migratory waders (comprising only a few species, perhaps), choose the right season to go to tidal mudflats and estuaries, or perhaps the local salt pans.

For some rare and endangered species you must search in very specific locations and be more than satisfied if you see a very small number of birds—or maybe only one.

However, if you want to see a large number of different species on a single day, you should consider something called the 'edge effect'. This is a place where one habitat meets another: where woodland meets grassland, or the forest meets the sea. A river flowing through dry country provides edge effect. Where two or more vegetation zones meet, the resulting diversity of plants and landforms provides a rich environment for many different bird species.

Variation in height above sea level can also provide edge effect as you walk out of a valley and up to the top of a hill. A large-scale example would be the Atherton Tableland above coastal Cairns, which gives climatic variation within the tropics. If you want something a little more bracing (and to see a few Keas), take a light-hearted stroll up Mount Cook from the beach to the summit!

An adult Australasian Grebe sets out across the lake surface of its
breeding territory in the late afternoon sun. Mungarannie,
South Australia

Habitat and bird communities

A discrete area of a single habitat type will contain recognisable groups of bird
species. Birds that frequent the same kind of habitat, and that are often found
together, can be called 'bird communities'. A patch of thick woodland in coastal
southern Queensland might contain doves, honeyeaters, robins and bowerbirds.
This subtropical woodland habitat type will not be suitable for all the members of
those bird families. You might see Bar-shouldered Dove, Lewin's Honeyeater, Rose
Robin and Satin Bowerbird. In drier woodland habitat a little further inland, the
same families might be represented by Peaceful Dove, Blue-faced Honeyeater,
Eastern Yellow Robin and Spotted Bowerbird. Some species will appear again and
again in several different habitat types. Three such widespread species are Nankeen
Kestrel, Willie Wagtail or New Zealand's Fantail.

The notion of 'community' has a connection with a defined habitat. An isolated
lake, for example, will contain a community of wetland birds that make use of every
variation of water level and marginal vegetation. If there is deep water as well as shallow, if there are clumping plants in the shallows, a variety of marginal plants, and
thick vegetation on the banks, there will be a correspondingly varied community of
birds foraging and breeding around the lake. Ducks, swans, grebes (dabchicks) and
others will form a community in and around a wetland, foraging at various water
levels and eating the variety of plants and insects found there. They are not usually in
direct competition with each other, and this is what 'community' is all about.

'Community' does not imply that the same individual birds, or species, are present throughout the year, but there is a good chance that a similar mix of species will be consistently recorded there. Any interference in the natural water level (whether by artificial flooding or drainage) will move the wetland further towards a monoculture. There will be less diversity in pond life or vegetation, and the birds will suffer accordingly.

When an area of habitat is reduced by clearing or 'development', its community of birds is subjected to intense pressure. In remnant patches of native vegetation, birds are crowded, forced out by new colonisers and exposed to predators from the surrounding land. A thriving, mixed community may sink to a few surviving species as their habitat is destroyed around them. If you frequently watch birds in the same area, you are likely to see a core group of perhaps thirty species again and again during a full year of birdwatching. But this group of species is not quite the same as a bird community, since your chosen area may cross several habitat boundaries.

Territory

A concept that is related to that of community, and which helps us to understand bird behaviour, is 'territory'. This refers to a piece of habitat that birds regard as their home ground and defend from others of the same species. Why do we need to understand territory? Because a bird engaged in defending its territory is likely to reveal its presence by vocal displays as it warns other birds to 'keep off', or advertises for a mate.

Territory, like habitat, has many variations. Birds such as Australasian Gannets, Straw-necked Ibis, Silver Gull (Red-billed Gull) and Sooty Tern, which breed in large colonies, may defend only the area of their nest. Laughing Kookaburras live in family parties that occupy and defend a territory of a hectare or more. The territory of a pair of Wedge-tailed Eagles or Powerful Owls can be even larger—up to many square kilometres in extent.

The Bell Miner is a territorial bird that lives in colonies. A major part of its food is the honeydew secreted by the lerps on eucalypt leaves. Each colony takes over a suitable patch of eucalypts and aggressively defends it against any other bird species. Other birds would eat the honeydew *and* the lerps, but the miners don't eat the lerps, they protect them. Too many lerps on a tree may kill the leaves and eventually the tree, so the patch of trees 'farmed' by the Bell Miners has to be large enough to sustain the colony without overstressing the trees. If the patch of eucalypt woodland is large enough, the Bell Miners will stay there for many

Little Penguins coming ashore at dusk. Twelve Apostles in western Victoria

Hummock grassland. Spinifex (*Triodia*) tussocks in the Simpson Desert, Northern Territory

years. But if there is intensive clearing around their territory, the patch may not be enough to sustain them and they will move away. Bell Miners are also known as Bellbirds and their clinking call is attractively bell-like. In Melbourne the sound of Bellbirds calling used to be a feature of many outer suburbs.

Habitat and distribution maps

All birdwatchers use the little distribution maps provided in field guides. But these maps can be quite misleading if used without realising that four types of distribution need to be considered: sedentary, migratory, nomadic and introduced.

Sedentary birds

Some birds range over an area of habitat that satisfies their physical needs all year. We call these 'sedentary' birds. If anything destroys their habitat they may not survive, because other suitable habitat nearby is already occupied and defended by birds of the same species.

At a very local level, birdwatchers should not make too many assumptions about sedentary birds. The scrub-wren or Tomtit you see constantly in your garden may *not* be the same individual every day, except perhaps in the breeding season when birds pair off and set up their own small territory. During the rest of the year, your garden may simply be within the home range of a number of scrub-wrens or Tomtits.

Migratory birds

In bird talk, the opposite of sedentary is migratory. Migratory birds annually fly considerable distances from their birthplace to avoid cold winters or hot summers, then return home again to breed. They often use the same kind of habitat (seashores and lake margins, for example) in each country, but in locations hundreds or even thousands of kilometres apart.

It might seem that these are more adaptable species than the sedentary birds but they, too, have specific feeding requirements. Some of these birds are very small. Imagine a sandpiper, only a hand's breadth from beak to tail tip, arriving from Siberia, close to the limits of its endurance. If it fails to find the right habitat and therefore the right food types at the end of its journey, it will perish.

Nomadic birds

Somewhere between sedentary and migratory birds, in classification terms, are the nomads. These are birds that travel widely to take advantage of seasonal changes in supplies of food. Many lorikeets and honeyeaters, particularly those in the drier country, regularly move to follow the flow of nectar in their favourite food plants.

After weather conditions that provide flooded pasture for breeding, large numbers of nomadic waterbirds may appear suddenly in an area. They have the capacity to breed rapidly whenever conditions are suitable. Species adapted to the dry inland of Australia have developed this quick breeding response to ensure their survival.

Sub-alpine open forest. Winter in the Australian Alps drives many bird species and individuals to undertake an altitudinal movement ('migration') to the coastal plains or drier hinterland. Snow Gum at Dinner Plain Hut, Victoria

Great-billed Heron. A four-month-old juvenile heron waits for its parents to return with food. The rufous plumage will moult to a more sombre brown colour as it becomes an adult. This bird (Australia's largest heron species) is in riverside (riparian) rainforest. Lower Daintree River, north Queensland

Grey Teal are well known for their ability to take advantage of ephemeral, or temporary, wetlands and may arrive in thousands after flooding rain. In periods of dry weather in Australia they may suddenly appear in New Zealand, where they now breed in numbers. In both countries their numbers appear to fluctuate because of their nomadic movements.

Another nomadic species is the Letter-winged Kite of the dry inland of Australia, which breeds in response to any periodic increase in Long-haired Rats, their principal food item.

The phenomena of nomadism and migration are reasons for using caution in interpreting distribution maps. A nomadic species, by its very nature, will not be found throughout its range at any time. You need to be aware of the factors that influence its nomadism.

Introduced birds

Some birds have naturally derived benefit from humankind's continuing interference with the natural environment. For example, Cattle Egrets have spread to every habitable continent because they benefit from the presence of grazing animals such as cattle and horses, which disturb insects and other food items in the grass.

New Zealand has suffered through introduction (acclimatisation) of many foreign birds, perhaps far more than Australia. Black Swans, Mallards and Canada Geese took to the waterways with gusto. Farmland-loving birds such as Pheasant, Wild Turkey, California Quail, Brown Quail, Rock Dove (Feral Pigeon), Eastern Rosella, Little Owl, Australian Magpie, Rook, Skylark, House Sparrow, Chaffinch, Redpoll, Goldfinch, Greenfinch, Yellowhammer, Cirl Bunting, Dunnock, Blackbird, Song Thrush, Starling and Myna, which were variously introduced from Europe, North America or Australia, have successfully colonised cleared farmland and its fringes.

As mentioned earlier, birds that easily adapt to life in cities, such as the Rock Dove, House Sparrow, Common Blackbird, Common Starling and Common Myna, have become more numerous with the urbanisation of the environment in both countries.

Birds that are able to take advantage of a wide variety of foods are not restricted to a single type of habitat. Starlings and mynas are two exceptional examples of species which, introduced to countries outside their original range, increased in some areas almost to plague proportions. Let's hope that no more non-indigenous bird species are deliberately introduced to any country.

Some great survivors in the bird world are those that alter the native vegetation, inadvertently creating the kind of habitat they prefer but driving out some of the original inhabitants in the process (just as humans tend to do). Although blackbirds, mynas and starlings are known to damage fruit crops, their ability to spread environmental weeds is not always appreciated. For example, blackberry is spread along creeks in southern Australia by the introduced blackbird, which eats the fruit and voids the seeds as it prospects for food in moist gullies, which suit both the blackbird and the blackberry.

Striated (Mangrove) Heron. This adult bird is fishing, staring into the water and occasionally slowly flattening itself from the edge of a rock, then reaching to strike at a fish from a low angle. Harbour breakwater, Townsville, Queensland

White-fronted Terns attaining white foreheads (frons) as the non-breeding season approaches. A few birds recently made nests on one of Tasmania's Furneaux Island group; subfossils in the soil show that breeding occurred there in the past. Paremata Estuary, Plimmerton, New Zealand

Many endemic birds also spread their own food plants by voiding the seeds. The Southern Cassowary, tropical fruit-eating doves and pigeons, Tui, silvereyes and Mistletoebird all 'plant' their favourite foods. It is only when environmental weeds have already been introduced into an area that the actions of these birds may also become a problem.

Vegetation and field descriptions

Another limitation of the distribution maps in field guides is that they do not show the details of vegetation. Within a species' range as drawn on a little distribution map, there may be large areas where the habitat is actually quite unsuitable.

You will also need to consider the field description, which hints at the species' abundance: 'common' or 'rare', or perhaps 'locally abundant'. Unless it is common throughout its range, you need to know something about a bird's habitat requirements in order to find it.

Distribution maps are about possibilities, not certainties. Knowledge of habitat types will greatly increase your chances of finding a particular species.

Let's take grebes as an example. Grebes are a cosmopolitan family of chunky sharp-beaked diving birds, the different species being distinguished from each other by markings on their heads. The birds have legs set far back on the body, and invariably walk poorly on land. They can be found in a variety of watery habitats, where they dive beneath the surface to feed. Their nests are constructed of aquatic vegetation, frequently floating and moored to some suitable obstacle or clump of protuberant plants.

Knowing all that, you would hardly expect to find grebes away from wetlands, but if you look at the distribution map for the Australasian (Little) Grebe, the whole of Australia and the northernmost peninsula (Northland) of New Zealand are coloured in. The maps are really saying that it is *possible* that, in *appropriate* habitat within the coloured area, you *may* see an Australasian Grebe.

Changes in habitat

Many vulnerable and endangered species are tied to a particular habitat or territory and are unable to adapt to change (or to the invasion of a more aggressive species). Very rapid habitat change is usually fatal.

Let's take an example from the honeyeater family. The Yellow-tufted Honeyeater is a beautiful olive bird in shades of golden yellow and olive green, with bright yellow ear tufts. Inland birds are slightly paler and may be nomadic, travelling to find blossoming eucalypts or other food plants. Coastal birds are darker in colour and are considered sedentary.

Some people regard the Helmeted Honeyeater not as a species but as a rare subspecies of the Yellow-tufted. It is obviously very closely related, but its plumage is darker again than either the inland or coastal races of Yellow-tufteds, and it has a crest or helmet of golden feathers on the front of its head. It is the bird emblem of the State of Victoria.

Not only is the Helmeted Honeyeater sedentary, it is tied to one location to such a degree that, despite an increasing restoration effort, it is in danger of extinction in the very near future. The Helmeted Honeyeater is found only in the Upper Yarra Region, a small area to the east of Melbourne, where it lives in the thick vegetation and water-loving eucalypts that grow along narrow watercourses.

As the region was cleared for timber and farming, only narrow remnant strips of vegetation were left along the riverbanks. This *might* have been just enough to support a viable bird population, but the change in habitat from woodland to open farmland allowed a more aggressive honeyeater, the Bell Miner, to invade the eucalypts and vie with the Helmeted Honeyeaters for the nectar, lerps and insects available. The Helmeted Honeyeater is now endangered, with a population of fewer than five hundred birds.

So here we have an example of one aggressive member of the honeyeater family (Bell Miner) whose invasion was detrimental to the survival of another member of the same family with similar food requirements (Helmeted Honeyeater).

A BIRD WALK IN NEW ZEALAND

This bird walk was undertaken by Ken in Plimmerton, approximately twenty-five kilometres north of Wellington, New Zealand. The season was late summer. He walked in a long rectangle from the home of his sister and her husband, taking three hours but travelling only about four kilometres.

We have chosen to share this walk with you because of the variety of different habitats that can be visited in one short journey. In fact, all the habitats of the area could be seen, and the walk was planned, from the topmost windows of the house.

The house is on a sharp north–south ridge with a view to the south over the approaches to Paremata Bay and Inlet and across to Mana Island offshore in a westerly direction. In the distance, on a clear day, the inter-island ferries can be seen crossing to and fro in Cook Strait, and beyond are the tall mountains of the South Island.

The vegetation is stunted and sculpted by the wind along the ridge, but there are several short deep creek valleys running down to the bay on the western side. These hold lush broad-leaf trees and shrubs and some introduced weeds and have an open understorey, like a rainforest in miniature. In one of these gullies, concrete steps run perhaps a hundred metres down to the beachfront. A street winds steeply down the spur to the main street of Plimmerton, on the narrow coastal plain.

The harbour behind the town is rather muddy, but there are many long tongues of folded rocks protruding into the sea. Behind these a narrow sandy beach has built up and an artificial sea wall along the esplanade keeps it all together—visually, anyway. Opposite the town are the highway and the railway, each carrying heavy traffic north towards Auckland and south to Wellington.

The gardens

After breakfast, I leave the house on foot at 8 a.m. on a sunny day in late summer. There is a light breeze that seems to change direction and is somewhat chilly.

A Kingfisher (Sacred Kingfisher; Kotare) is on the telephone line, and a dozen or more Silvereyes (Tauhou) are in a trimmed hebe hedge behind a white picket fence in a neighbour's garden. I can hear two Australian Magpies carolling down below, near the railway line. The little chirruping calls of four European Goldfinches attract my attention, their yellow wing patches briefly visible when they are close to me, and I watch their flicking undulating flight along the road to a tall conifer.

Standing at the head of the steps, with the morning sun over my left shoulder, I have a lovely view over the inlet, beach and rocks to the island and the sea beyond. I lean my elbows on a handrail for binocular steadiness in the breeze, and gaze around the area. Six habitats are below me: the ocean and bay; the dense patch of forest immediately to my front and right; a scattering of houses by the road, with gardens, power poles and TV aerials all available for scrutiny; a foreshore with sand and rocks; and the estuary. Beyond the ridge is the shopping centre and the flax swamp. I know that each habitat may contain something different in the way of birds.

The sea

Out over the sea, a few widely spread Australasian Gannets can be seen, and a White-faced Heron suddenly flies along the face of the ridge towards the yacht club. Terns, small and white, are flying over the bay, not clear enough for *reliable* identification yet. Far out beyond them and barely visible to the eye, tiny black shapes rising and falling where the sea meets the sky suggest a flock of feeding shearwaters.

The forest

I move down the steps towards the esplanade. Several Fantails (Piwakawaka) are singing in the gully, with a female Common Blackbird down in the litter and a tiny, red-eyed Grey Warbler (Riroriro) moving around and through a small-leafed shrub. Further down, a juvenile Shining Cuckoo (Pipiwharauroa), with tinges of brown in the wings and patchy bars across the breast, sits under the canopy on a thin twig. It calls persistently, but no bird comes near to feed it.

Urban houses

Four Common Starlings are sunning themselves on a TV aerial, but no other birds are seen down amongst the houses.

Foreshore

Many young Red-billed Gulls (Tarapunga: dull reddish bill, legs and feet) and a pair of Black-billed (Buller's) Gulls (black eye ring, bill, legs and feet) are on the sandy beach when I reach it. Black-backed Gulls (Karoro) of different ages are standing or sitting on the sand, the adults with yellow bills and a red spot on the lower mandible only, greenish legs and feet, plain white tails. A few are quarrelling and occasionally flying around the rocks, only to return within thirty seconds or so to the same patch.

Towards the seaward end of the wonderfully parallel rock strata is a pair of Variable Oystercatchers (Torea or Toreapango), and a couple of hundred closely packed small terns. These soon resolve themselves into White-fronted Terns (Tara), just about the most common species in New Zealand. Some are in full breeding plumage with jet black foreheads; those with speckled white foreheads are entering the non-breeding or wintering plumage. Beyond them stands a solitary Caspian Tern (Taranui), its large red beak and great size very obvious and easily identifiable.

Estuary

I walk southward beyond the rocks to the estuary and shopping centre. At the inlet, feeding over the muddy surface as the tide comes slowly in, and behind the various shops (the fish shop is *my* favourite) is a pair of White-faced Herons and several Black-winged Stilts (Pied; Poaka), including two juveniles with smudgy grey crowns. A distant lone brown dumpy little wader with few distinguishing marks is taking me quite a while to decipher. One Little Shag (Little Pied Cormorant; Kauwaupaka) stands watchfully on a weed-covered outlet pipe near the sea wall, and more White-fronted Terns dip low to feed over the rippling water as they fly to join the cluster of terns already on the rocks.

The wader takes speedy flight and I have a quick but clear view of a buff-yellow face and neck and part of one faded chest band. It is an immature Banded Dotterel (Double-banded Plover).

Shopping centre and flax swamp

Inland to the east, around the shops and railway station, are Common Starlings, a few House Sparrows, and many feral Rock Pigeons (Rock Dove in Australia). Behind the rail yards is a sports oval and more houses in well-established gardens. Some large exotic trees have many Common Starlings in and about them.

Below the railway line embankment is a long, narrow flax swamp. The flax swamp holds deep water, invisible until I step on to the verge and my boots suddenly squelch into wet mud. I had planned to walk through the middle of the swamp, thinking 'Fernbird', and had checked the distribution descriptions in my New Zealand field guide to see if it could be there. My 'research' indicated that the species occurs in a narrow belt southward on the west coast of the North Island and just *possibly* could have extended to the little flax swamp at Plimmerton. On a good day, perhaps, but not today.

In the swamp, several Pukeko (Purple Swamphens) are obvious. They rapidly take avoiding action, trotting off and flicking their white undertail triangles towards me. Many pairs of House Sparrows and two Dunnocks (Hedge Sparrows) are in the flax and in gorse bushes and other rank vegetation at the margins.

I scramble up the steepest part of the ridge, then take a track up a cleared grassy slope with burnt gorse stumps. A pair of introduced Skylarks rises as I pass.

As I follow the street along the ridge top towards the house, the four Goldfinches are feeding in dried thistle heads in the lane behind the fences. The Kingfisher is visible, but a hundred metres further down the road, and the Silvereyes are still in the neighbour's hebe hedge. The morning stroll is over.

This walk is one during which Ken visited a series of clearly defined habitats one after the other, seeing a few species characteristic of each, and a few birds that are likely to be seen anywhere. Three hours later, several of the birds were still where he first saw them.

The close-packed nests of breeding Australasian Gannets in part of the famous Cape Kidnappers gannetry. This is also a good example of coastal cliffs and seas. North Island, New Zealand

CHAPTER THREE

Family likenesses

We have been discussing the advantage of learning about different habitat types so that you can anticipate which birds you are likely to find where. But what if you suddenly find yourself in a beaut place that combines two or three different habitats, each clearly so rich with birds that you are temporarily overwhelmed? Unexpectedly travelling in this bird-rich area, you have had no time to 'bone up' on the species you might expect to see.

This is where family recognition comes to your aid. Habitat preference was one way of filtering the birds to help us identify them. Family is another.

In this chapter we will look at how family similarities of general appearance and behaviour can help you to recognise individual bird species. Nature of movement on the ground or in trees, foraging and then actual eating techniques, calls, and flight mannerisms are the main behavioural clues you will use to identify birds.

Families and habitats

As a general rule we can say that each different species within a bird family is adapted to a slightly different habitat. This adaptation contributes to the survival of the whole family, but may not necessarily ensure the survival of any individual species.

It means that members of a family, having evolved from a common stock, will have recognisable similarities in shape, behaviour and patterns of colour. Familiarity with families is an important aid to birdwatching identification because you can quickly turn to the right page in your field guide to identify the species. (The colour-illustrated 'Key to Families' in the front of Simpson & Day's *Field Guide to the Birds of Australia* is a useful aid.)

What is a family? Let's look at Kingfishers as an example.

The Laughing Kookaburra (Jackass or Kingfisher) and the more northern Blue-winged Kookaburra belong to the kingfisher family Halcyonidae. They are easily recognisable in shape, having large heads, a strong sword-like beak and a short blunt tail, and are known for their raucous calls.

Laughing Kookaburras are easy to spot because they have a habit of perching on posts, wires, or bare branches, from which they plunge to the ground to capture worms, skinks and so on. They are slow to fly and, except in direct level flight, not particularly agile in the air. They nest in tree hollows.

Kookaburras are the largest local members of the Halcyonidae. Their immediate smaller relatives include the Sacred (just called Kingfisher in New Zealand), the Red-backed and Forest Kingfishers, which have the same heavy-beaked profile and look like pint-sized, dapper versions of the Laughing Kookaburra.

Although called kingfishers, some of the family are found in open woodland and their diet may include a variety of small creatures other than fish. The large kookaburras eat a multitude of invertebrates, plus snakes, frogs, lizards, small mammals and birds, nestlings and eggs.

Within a family there are usually similarities in the way in which members use their habitat for feeding or nesting, as well as similarities of stance, calls or other behaviours that can assist with identification. The small kingfishers have quick chattering but repetitive calls, less 'ponderous' than those of the two kookaburras.

One day you are standing at the edge of a patch of mulga shrubland when you catch a glimpse of a small bird diving to the ground and returning to disappear into the leaves of a tree. Your knowledge of family behaviour suggests kingfishers, whistlers and robins. However, you know that robins tend to perch on the sides of trunks and the bare parts of a tree, and that a dive to the ground is a fairly uncommon behaviour for the whistlers. You suspect the bird may be a small kingfisher, and stare hopefully into the leaves for several minutes.

During this time you are mentally running through the kingfisher family in your mind, and you are pretty certain that in this thin mulga shrubland in Meekathara, Western Australia, the bird will be a Sacred or Red-backed Kingfisher.

So, when it bursts from the leaves and darts swiftly across your head to another tree, you know what to look for: flat, straight flight, strong beak, short tail. Yes, it's a kingfisher. Distinguishing marks? It moved too swiftly to see enough detail. Ah, well, put it down to experience. But every observation you make will add to your knowledge.

FAMILIES

Family classifications are derived from evolutionary relationships (which is why sequences change as more details of their genetic structure are discovered from DNA work). However, each family does not necessarily have exclusive use of a given behaviour pattern. Bird species from quite different families may develop similar specialised anatomy. For example, brush tongues have developed in lorikeets, honeyeaters and chats, woodswallows and silvereyes.

Other bird families use similar behaviour to take advantage of similar habitat types. Examples are the bark-foraging behaviour of treecreepers, sittellas and Brown Creeper, and tree-hollow nesting of some parrots, owls, Australian Owlet-nightjar, treecreepers, some pardalotes, Yellowhead, House Sparrow, Gouldian Finch, Tree Martin, Common Starling and Common Myna. This is called convergent evolution.

Other families show a range of behaviours across different habitats (ducks, waders, honeyeaters, finches), which could be called evolutionary radiation.

Family likeness: three tree-kingfishers compared. This adult Blue-winged Kookaburra
has dark striations on the crown, typical of the eastern and northern Australian race.
The edge of a brown tail just shows that it is a female bird. The prominent bill is
'boat-shaped'.

Largest of the tree-kingfishers is the well-known Laughing Kookaburra of eastern continental Australia. It occurs in a wide range of habitats. Introduced into south-west of Western Australia, Kangaroo Island in South Australia and Tasmania, including Flinders Island. Also to New Zealand. This is an adult.

The small Red-backed Kingfisher is virtually a miniature replica of its two larger relatives. This is a prominent bird of Australia's more arid and tropical zones. Mungo National Park, central southern New South Wales

Key to families

Worldwide there are more than eight thousand known bird species, divided into about a hundred families.

While all birds have some similar basic behaviours (they may walk, hop, fly, hover, swim, dive or climb), different families have different, identifiable ways of doing these actions. Penguins tend to walk on land in an upright posture. Magpie Geese, whistling-ducks and shelducks may hold themselves more upright than others of the duck family. Most herons stand and perch upright, as do cormorants and shags, and the Darter. On the other hand, the stance of terns on the ground tends to be horizontal, as does that of many ducks. Flocks of cockatoos feeding on the ground have a horizontal stance.

Gradually, with experience, you will absorb family similarities and differences into your everyday birdwatching. Awareness, a conscious looking for trends, is important.

In Simpson & Day's 'Key to Families', the stance and shape of typical family members are illustrated in colour, and familiarity with these family types will assist your early attempts at identification. Families placed close together in field guides (and other texts that follow the latest accepted checklist sequences) are considered to have greater similarities than those placed far apart in these books. For example, herons are like egrets and bitterns and *somewhat* like ibis, spoonbills, storks and cranes. Penguins are unlike hawks or parrots, robins or saddlebacks.

The 'jizz' of a bird

Let's say that you have identified your first cuckoo, a Fan-tailed Cuckoo. Next time you see a cuckoo, you are able to recognise it as a member of the cuckoo family (Cuculidae) even though you may not be quite sure of its species. What are the factors that tell you 'cuckoo' so readily?

The bird is perching on a dead branch of a tree. It has an air of alert concentration, a 'wide-eyed, self-conscious' look. Its body is held vertically and the colour of its plumage blends into the bark. It looks as if it has recently had a 'haircut'.

This description is far from scientific. It even includes anthropomorphism (applying human emotions to wildlife), frowned on by some people. But the description certainly gives us some feeling for the essential cuckoo, some combination of behaviour and inner character (personality) that can be summed up in the word 'jizz'.

'Jizz' is a useful word in birdwatching because it explains the unexplainable. When ornithologists use this word, they can deny that they are using emotions or their 'sixth sense' to identify a creature.

ORIGIN OF 'JIZZ'

'Jizz' is possibly a phonetic spelling of GISS (General Impression of Size and Shape), used by pilots when learning aircraft recognition in World War II.

This adult Fan-tailed Cuckoo is perched in precisely the 'vertical' posture of the cuckoo family that we have described. Cuckoos have a lovely tapered body shape when in this position. Note the yellow eye skin (the Brush Cuckoo's eye skin is grey). Fraser National Park, central Victoria

'Jizz' encapsulates everything about a bird that makes it uniquely recognisable. 'Jizz' includes more than shape and colour, it includes all the added characteristic behaviour and movement or, if you like, essence or inner character, of the species. Some of this character is created by the facial patterns. Whitefaces always look 'sad'; White-browed Scrubwrens 'frown and look angry', Yellow Wattlebirds look like elderly ladies with pendant earrings.

Back to cuckoos.

The widely known Willie Wagtail is a favourite bird, its scolding rattle instantly identifiable. All members of the insectivorous Australasian 'flycatcher' group wag their tails from side to side, unlike the Northern Hemisphere 'motacillid' wagtails, which wag theirs up and down. Dry open woodland, Chiltern, north-east central Victoria

The larger cuckoos frequently perch on the outside dead sticks of trees or on fences, and tend to pose vertically. Of course there are exceptions, such as a Pallid Cuckoo standing horizontally on a fence post, butchering a hairy caterpillar.

Cuckoos' eyes seem large and round and staring because they are often surrounded by a coloured eye ring, giving the 'wide-eyed' look you noticed; and the impression of alertness comes from the upright stance.

Most of this you may never consciously describe to yourself. You simply 'recognise' the bird as a cuckoo. The study of family characteristics and behaviour, together with a little field experience, gives you the 'jizz'. Once you have the bird's 'jizz' in your memory you really feel you 'know' the bird.

To go further into 'jizz', the Pallid Cuckoo has rather a mournful, resentful look, created by a combination of a descending eye stripe and a 'beak in the air'. So, at the same instant when you see a possible cuckoo (a vertically perched plain bird of the right size), you recognise the 'mournful look' of a Pallid Cuckoo.

Only after checking plumage details, however, and perhaps hearing it call, will you confirm the sighting and write the record in your notebook. Positively identify every bird (see page 69)—and check the bird *again* if another opportunity occurs.

There are so many examples of family behaviours that lead to quick identification that we cannot cover them all here, but you will soon observe many for yourself. Cuckoo-shrikes and trillers of the family Campephagidae refold their wings when alighting, leading to the cuckoo-shrike's old name of 'Shufflewing'. Such descriptive names are useful aids to memory. Ravens (family Corvidae) are part of a family of large, black birds with loud harsh calls, a group that is familiar to non-birdwatchers as 'crows'. Of the three species, the Little Ravens can be identified by their tendency to flick their wing tips when calling.

'Seabirds'

'Seabirds' is a broad group word covering birds of several distinct families. Many are coastal seabirds, living (more or less) in shallow seas and often within sight of land. Some penguins, Australasian Gannet, most cormorants and shags, Australian Pelican, and some gulls and terns are a few examples.

Before we go on, an expression you may sometimes read or hear is 'pelagic'. Pelagic species are those that live their lives almost entirely at sea, returning to land only for breeding purposes. Since many species breed on the coast or on offshore islands, it is not always necessary to go offshore to see them, but 'pelagic trips' are undertaken by seabird enthusiasts who hire a boat to take them to the edge of the continental shelf to increase their chances of seeing the rarer albatrosses, petrels or terns.

The birds they see will depend on season, latitude and local weather conditions. These include *some* family members of the penguins, albatrosses, petrels, storm-petrels, tropicbirds and frigatebirds, skuas and jaegers, and certain gulls and terns. We won't list the many family names; you can look them up!

The tropical frigatebirds (family Fregatidae) are interesting. Long-winged, like a hang-glider in flight, the adult males and females of our three species have similar, yet slightly differing plumages, and the series of identifying white patches on the black underside of the body is confusing at first. This is a small group whose markings need to be swotted-up for true certainty.

Frigatebirds frequently soar on tropical thermals and associate themselves about the edges of cyclonic weather systems. The birds feed by snatching food items from the sea surface, and sometimes swoop to drink on the wing at freshwater coastal pools. They have a well-developed habit of pursuing other seabirds (cormorants, boobies, terns, noddies) and forcing them to disgorge the fish or other food caught. The frigatebird seizes the food as it falls, then makes off. Gulls, skuas and jaegers have a similar robbing behaviour, which is called 'kleptoparasitism'.

Raptors

Now we come to an example of two families that are easily recognisable in a general sense, but not quite so easy to identify individually. They are the ospreys, hawks and eagles (family Accipitridae), and the falcons (family Falconidae). There is enough variation of plumage and behaviour in these two families for enthusiasts to devote most of their birdwatching lives to them. There is also a substantial literature. We must warn you that if you become fascinated by raptors it may rapidly turn into an obsession. Totally unscientific research we have carried out suggests that men are more likely to become obsessed with raptors than women are. Exceptions exist of course, but . . . something to do with the hunter-gatherer difference, perhaps?

The common group name for these hunters is 'raptors' (it requires less knowledge to look up into the sky and say 'Ah, a raptor' than to say 'There goes a Brown Goshawk in second-year plumage'). The cry 'Raptor coming!' is common in birdwatching circles because frequently they are quite large, distinctive in shape and mannerisms and visible at a good distance if high enough in the air. Thus alerted, the birdwatchers prepare to give the bird their full attention if it comes overhead.

A well-known raptor behaviour is hunting for prey by hovering, although few raptors actually hunt in this way. Black-shouldered Kites hover over grasslands as they search for small rodents. The Letter-winged Kite does the same at night, hunting the Long-haired Rat in central Australia.

Harriers make long, low searching flights over wetlands, grasslands and crops. White-bellied Sea-Eagles perch on tall trees beside water and swoop down to grab fish and other aquatic prey (sea snakes, small turtles, occasionally a penguin) from just below the surface of the water.

The falcons differ from the rest of the raptors in that they do not grab their prey and crush it with strong claws. Falcons (which include hobbies and kestrels) have strong beaks and kill their prey by severing the neck. They have long, narrow pointed wings and are very agile and fast in flight. The smallest falcon in Australia is the Nankeen Kestrel.

One other behaviour that divides the falcons from the 'hawks' is that they do not build their own nests but nest on cliff edges, or use tree hollows, or the disused nests of other species.

The widespread but comparatively rare New Zealand Falcon (Karearea) has three regional plumages, and each has a local regional common name. Body size varies, as does feather colouring, but intergrading of the three occurs. The habitat type preferred by each seems to dictate where the various forms are found.

THE 'WHITE' GREY GOSHAWK

Some individuals in the Grey Goshawk population of Australia are absolutely pure white, but are not albino. They are often called 'white phase' but this is misleading as the colour does not change (as in 'phased out') but remains throughout life. The preferred term is white morph.

The white plumage is produced by a recessive gene, so two White Goshawks will breed true. These white birds now predominate on the north and south coasts of Australia, including Tasmania. On the east coast and inland the true Grey Goshawk is more often seen.

Occasionally a pair of Grey morph Goshawks produce a white morph chick, but each colour is always true. You will never find a mixed grey and white bird.

Rails

The rail family (Rallidae) includes the large swamphens, moorhens, coots and native-hens that are common to many lakes and swamps. Most have a characteristic way of flicking their short tails upwards as they walk or swim.

Many others in the rail family are small and very secretive, hiding in thick vegetation near water, and often a birdwatcher's sight of them is limited to a brief glimpse as they dash across a gap in the reeds. Patience and absolute stillness are necessary if you want to see them well.

Plovers and dotterels

Members of this family (Charadriidae), which includes the lapwings, have had their common names changed around so often that *we* have become confused. If you are just starting out on your birdwatching career you will, of course, learn the new names and wonder why other birdwatchers stick to the old ones.

These birds are all plump-bodied and round-headed, with high foreheads, large eyes, and a stout bill shorter than the head. Plovers and dotterels have a characteristic 'run and stop' method of feeding, which is attractively reminiscent of clockwork toys. They move away from the observer in a broadly circular direction, returning to the same feeding or nesting place. The Inland Dotterel of Australia is the only one that has adapted to arid areas. The bill of New Zealand's world-famous Wrybill always has a right-hand bend. It is suited to clipping aquatic invertebrates from the undersides of river pebbles.

Lapwings are larger birds of the same general shape, some species more nomadic than others. The Masked Lapwing (Spur-winged Plover) is a common bird of farmland in southern Australia and is a comparatively recent arrival in New Zealand. These birds are strongly territorial in the breeding season and in large cities may choose apparently unsuitable nesting sites such as flat factory roofs, supermarket carparks or sporting fields. When they fly at night, their repetitive, cackling call betrays their presence.

Cockatoos and parrots

Cockatoos and parrots, the Cacatuidae and Psittacidae families, all have an easily recognisable 'parrot' shape, with short necks and strong, hooked bills.

Cockatoos tend to have crests, which they raise in anger or excitement. Included in this group are the very familiar Sulphur-crested and Major Mitchell's (Pink) Cockatoos, the Galah, the corellas and the Cockatiel. All have been adopted for human companionship. Most feed on the ground, and several are regarded by grain farmers as pests because they feed on cereal crops.

Gang-gang Cockatoos move quietly around in the treetops, hardly revealing their presence except for occasional twigs, leaves or seed-cases that fall on your head as you search for them. It is always a surprise when, after you have located one or two Gang-gangs feeding above you, a disturbance sends a dozen hitherto unnoticed birds out of the same tree.

Black-Cockatoos are magnificent, large birds with slow-motion flight and mournful cries. Many of them feed on the tiniest casuarina and eucalypt seeds. These large long-lived birds need large nest-hollows in mature trees. Tree-clearing for agricultural and urban development has seriously affected their breeding capacity and several species are now in decline.

Lorikeets are noisy bright-green parrots with various underwing and facial patterns of red, yellow and blue. They have brush-tipped tongues and feed on nectar and pollen. Some also eat fruit and soft grains, which does not make them popular with orchardists and farmers. They are nomads, appearing suddenly in a district in order to take advantage of seasonal bursts of flowers or fruit.

Fig-Parrots are the smallest Australian parrots, with limited distribution in rainforest on the east coast, where they may also be found in gardens with soft-fruit trees. They are far more often heard than seen, except when flying high and fast as tiny silhouettes.

More members of the parrot family are described in this chapter's bird walk.

> ### FAMILY OR GROUP NAMES ALLUDING TO BEHAVIOUR OR SHAPE
> Mound-builders, Shearwaters, Diving-Petrels, Darters, Swamphens, Spoonbills, Plains-wanderer, Turnstones, Sandpipers, Stone-curlews, Oystercatchers, Stilts, Swifts, Bee-eaters, Rollers, Lyrebirds, Treecreepers, Thornbills, Honeyeaters, Logrunners, Whipbirds, Whistlers, Flycatchers, Fantails, Figbirds, Bowerbirds, Trillers, Butcherbirds, Mud-nesters, Wagtails, Warblers, Weavers

Treecreepers

Treecreepers have recently been reconsidered in the evolutionary sequence as a result of DNA work, and are now regarded as being fairly close in ancestry to the lyrebirds and scrub-birds.

Yellow-tufted Honeyeater, relative of the endangered Helmeted Honeyeater. Licola, Victoria

Yellow-plumed Honeyeater. The adult Yellow-plumed Honeyeater (sometimes called the 'Mallee Honeyeater') arrives with an insect for a fledgling. Mungo National Park, New South Wales

Striped Honeyeater, a bird of eastern temperate Australia, sun-basking with separated feathers.

They are relatively plain brown birds with strong voices and tend to look for food on the ground or on main trunks and branches. They *tend* to begin each foraging episode from the lower parts of trees.

They hold their bodies in an upright position, leaning back on their tails as they hop up vertical tree trunks. They hop, rather than walk, with feet together. Since they are usually birds of trunks and branches, they need to be distinguished from the smaller, short-tailed sittellas, which have a tendency to forage downwards from the top of the trees.

Honeyeaters

Another large family is the honeyeaters, the Meliphagidae. They all have a brush-tipped tongue with which they can collect fluids, and their name and behaviour would seem to be self-explanatory. But life is never so simple, is it? As a beginner, you can watch some honeyeater species, such as the spinebill or Tui, and know, from their behaviour at flowers, that they are feeding on nectar and are patently of the honeyeater family. However, if you were trying to work out the family of the White-naped Honeyeater as you watched it probing its short beak into the bark of a eucalypt, searching for insects, the word 'honeyeater' might not spring to mind.

Honeyeaters can be roughly divided into three groups, and it is worth a little study of their habits before you attempt to identify them in the field. Species such as spinebills and the New Holland Honeyeater tend to feed mainly on nectar and can be called 'nectarivorous'. Most honeyeaters have a very varied diet, but are mainly 'insectivorous', feeding on honeydew, lerps and insects. The Spiny-cheeked and Singing Honeyeaters are known to eat large amounts of fruit in season, and are part of the 'frugivorous' group.

Honeyeaters have adapted to every terrestrial habitat in Australia and some in New Zealand. Although they all have a brush-tipped tongue with which they suck nectar and collect pollen from flowers, their behaviour varies according to habitat, season and the local supply of other foods. Male Stitchbirds and Bellbirds (New Zealand), for example, are thought to take more nectar and fruit than their females, which eat more insects.

Just don't assume that 'honeyeaters' live only on nectar. Particularly when breeding, honeyeaters take large numbers of insects, which provide a high-protein diet for their developing nestlings.

Many honeyeaters move around to take advantage of seasonal variations in nectar-flow and insect availability, so you may often see a group of several different species travelling together. Their movements are strongly associated with the flowering of native plants. If a region can provide a year-long supply of food, the honeyeaters need not travel far.

In your home garden, remember that, however much you would like to encourage honeyeaters to become permanent residents, it is detrimental to provide an artificial nectar source on which the birds become dependent. Planting a group of native bushes that will flower in different months of the year will be of more benefit to the birds in the long run.

White-browed Woodswallow. This immaculately plumaged male is drinking from a temporary rainwater pool. Woodswallows from now on may be thought of as specialised butcherbirds. Chiltern, north-east central Victoria

Thrushes

The 'true' Thrush family includes Common Blackbird and Song Thrush, sweet-singing species that have been introduced into our region from Europe. The Blackbird is an almost universally recognised shape and size, and for that very purpose forms a reference species in many bird texts, this one included.

The Bassian and Russet-tailed Thrushes of Australia are large brownish thrushes, most frequently encountered in damp to wet forest and rainforest. They can easily be distinguished from Blackbirds because they do not hop, but run in short bursts along the ground, heads held low and poking forward, and then freeze. If they are aware of your presence they will hold their position for as long as twenty minutes (we timed a Bassian Thrush in our garden).

More bird families are described in later chapters.

Remember that you will rarely have to distinguish between *all* the birds in one family at one time. A little study of habitats and distribution maps will ease your burden considerably.

You might go on a long and costly expedition to a north-west Australian tidal mangrove forest to see a White-breasted Whistler, but when you get there, you must be able to separate it from Rufous Whistlers, since they might also be there. However, if a Golden Whistler also turns up in your mangrove forest, your distribution maps (and small differences in size and plumage) will tell you that it *must* be a Mangrove Golden Whistler.

Distribution maps will tell you which birds are *unlikely* to be seen in a given region, as well as giving you a hint as to what you may find there.

A huddle of Apostlebirds on a branch on a cold afternoon. These are all members of the same family group, a co-operative breeding species and extremely sociable within their family. They all look alike. Mungo National Park, New South Wales

A BIRD WALK IN GULPA FOREST

*When you go for a bird walk, you will try to see as many species as you can. We think it
becomes more interesting if you also set yourself a special task.*

*We set out on this morning walk to study different bird families that live in and use the same
general habitat. It turned out that quite a lot of comparisons were possible in one morning in
Gulpa Forest in southern New South Wales.*

We passed a long low green board with the legend 'Gulpa Forest' as we drove south-east
from Mathoura, heading towards Picnic Point, the Edwards River, Moira Lake, the Gulpa
Creek and the Murray River in southern central New South Wales. A Peaceful Dove was
preening on the post at one end of the board.

Beyond it, the road broadened and opened out into private farmland to the north and
Red Gum forest, heavily exploited, to the south. It was a sunny, slightly breezy day. We
parked the car in the sparse shade of a small roadside Red Gum and set out on foot over
the long sand dune that parallels the road at this point. Eaten almost bare by stock, it
carried a broken cover of regenerating everlasting daisies, copper burrs and little patches
of a scrubby dark succulent.

Along the crest of the ridge were some scattered clumps of wind-blasted Murray Pines
and She-oaks. Broken branches and heavy bark littered the ground under every tree. Along
the top of the ridge an electric transmission line ran on tall poles.

Down in the hollow beyond the dune was a broad clay-soil plain of samphire and
numerous patches of Black Box, a eucalypt that prefers less regular flooding than the
River Red Gums. This is a low-rainfall region, but seasonal flooding of the adjacent river
systems delivers plenty of water through the forests in a good year.

By lunchtime we had seen a lot of nice birds.

We had seen a small flock of Australian Pelicans circling at a very great height, two
Whistling Kites, two Nankeen Kestrels, several Rainbow Bee-eaters, Brown Treecreepers,
Noisy and Little Friarbirds, Blue-faced Honeyeaters, Magpie-larks, a family of White-
winged Choughs, Australian Magpies, some unidentified ravens in the far distance, and a
small flock of Common Starlings.

Amongst the small insectivores we saw were a pair of Striated Pardalotes, some
Weebills, a small party of Chestnut-rumped Thornbills, many Yellow-rumped and four
Buff-rumped Thornbills, and about nine Southern Whitefaces. For convenience this
particular group of small birds can be referred to as the 'acanthizids', which represents a
useful group name for all those species (about fifty Australia-wide) now contained in the
recently reorganised family Pardalotidae.

Down in the hollow behind the dune we also found a brilliant set of male robins
(family Petroicidae) amongst some fallen Black Box trees and litter. We saw Red-capped
Robin, Hooded Robin, Flame Robin, all with their attendant females, and in addition a
pair of Jacky Winters.

For a while, it was hard to look beyond the cockatoos (family Cacatuidae). Every few
minutes, more would come over: Sulphur-crested Cockatoos, Little Corellas, Long-billed

Corellas and heaps of Galahs. It wasn't even necessary to raise our heads because the calls of these four species are different. The rippling, slightly musical calls of the two corellas are rather similar, but the raucous Sulphur-crested Cockatoos and shrill Galahs are obvious at all times. Corellas are more 'level' in flight than the Sulphur-crested and the Galahs, which often tend to roll around the sky, rocking from side to side. Galahs often fly in close pairs.

Unexpectedly, Cockatiels went through in a tight flock—just six brown birds flying hard, showing off their wonderful white wing flashes. We heard them coming, alerted by the ringing calls. The crests, being pressed to the head, are not really visible in flight. Unless you're in the know, Cockatiels in flight, and in much of their general behaviour, look very much like a group of long-tailed parrots.

There were several members of the parrot family Psittacidae, too. We had seen little groups of Red-rumped Parrots amongst the Red Gums all along the road, often rising from the roadside to perch in them as we drove by. The bright green heads and yellow bellies of the males were very visible in contrast to the drab greenish-brown female of each pair. A common and easily identified small parrot in south-eastern Australia, the males have a large bright red rump, hidden when feeding on the ground, but exposed as they rise away from you.

A pair of bright green Australian Ringnecks flew along the roadside for a few moments, then turned into the dense forest. Several Eastern Rosellas were perched on the fence further down the road, where the dune begins to level out near a wheat field.

We walked to where dark brown-coloured Blue Bonnets were flying amongst the She-oaks and Murray Pines. Sometimes they flew across to perch on the electricity cable or dropped in pairs to the ground, only to fly back to their favoured trees when alarmed.

A group of Yellow Rosella pairs, pale yellowish in the sunlight, with dark blue upper wings and tails, arrived in a Red Gum, perched briefly, then flew on when they saw us standing quietly almost at their eye level. Yellow Rosellas are a pale subspecies of the 'blue-cheeked' Crimson Rosella complex. Technically Crimson Rosellas, it is still best to enter them in your field notes as 'Yellow Rosellas', so that no ambiguity can arise in your records later on. For any species that has colour variations, careful records are especially important near the boundaries between different forms.

All these broad-tailed parrots fly along in gentle undulation, rising slightly as the wingbeats take effect, and falling as they progress momentarily with closed wings. Distinctive features of all these cockatoos and parrots in the field are the constant maintenance of obvious pairs, little dark eyes in broad round heads, the distinctly solid decurved bills, and the perpetual chatter, whether at rest or in motion. Over a three-hour period we actually saw ten species of the psittacids (the group name for the cockatoos and parrots) in one small patch of dry forest. A feature of the Australian bush is that there are always several species of cockatoos and parrots no matter where you choose to go.

Next we looked at three species of the family Halcyonidae, the kingfishers. Sacred Kingfishers were calling from the Red Gums across the road to the south of us. A Red-backed Kingfisher and a pair of the much larger Laughing Kookaburras were perched on the powerlines, not very far apart. The miniature shape of the small Red-backed alongside the hulking Kookaburras made their family relationship obvious in spite of the difference in size. In particular we looked at the squared-away heads, the prominent, pointed but bulging bill (sometimes called boat-shaped), the large round eye set in a burglar's mask of black or brown. The relative postures of the two species were practically identical. Here were two birds, differently coloured, differently sized, but each perched on a cable, each peering down intently for long periods, each occasionally flying down to grab some squirming little morsel from the sand, each returning to whack it thoroughly on the wire, gulp it down and carefully clean the beak.

The Azure, an additional kingfisher species of the related family Alcedinidae, was not on the dune but three kilometres down the road, flitting up and down the banks of the Gulpa Creek. We found it later in the day; we hadn't anticipated seeing another kingfisher, but there it was—a rich blue gem in the sunlight. Structural differences do exist between the two families but are not very obvious. Azure Kingfishers (and the very tropical Little Kingfisher) exclusively fish and catch invertebrates in pools and creeks for food. They both have proportionately longer and slightly thinner (less 'boat-shaped') bills.

Another fine selection of birds prominent on this dune ridge were a black-backed pair of Australian Magpies and two butcherbird species. A female Grey Butcherbird was taking tiny lizards in the scrubby hollow and a pair of the larger Pied Butcherbirds foraged in the Red Gum saplings across the road from the car.

These three species are members of the recently restructured family Artamidae, which also includes currawongs and woodswallows. Within the hour more members of the family arrived. Six White-breasted Woodswallows began hawking insects over the ridge, flying steeply upward, turning sharply and gliding down to the power lines, or circling around in flat spirals.

Magpies and butcherbirds tend to glide in long straight flight, with the wings held practically flat. Woodswallows glide in the same manner but in circles. Coincidentally, all the Artamidae we saw on the dune have bluish-white bill bases with black hooked tips, and white rumps, although the other woodswallows do not. The three currawongs also in this family have black bills and do not glide quite so 'flatly' or neatly, and only the Pied Currawong has a white rump.

The family Hirundinidae was well represented at the Gulpa Creek dune system. From time to time during the morning we noticed small numbers of Welcome Swallows, Fairy Martins and Tree Martins flying about, usually close to the ground, all appearing and disappearing between trees, vanishing for a while, returning again . . .

We found this a very interesting study of bird families.

CHAPTER FOUR

Identification

So far we have discussed identification broadly, with many generalisations. We now come to the nitty-gritty of bird identification by physical features.

Colour is where many birdwatchers begin. Colour attracts your eye and stimulates your interest. Just as in gardening the novice is often attracted by plants with bright red or yellow flowers, so in birdwatching the Purple Swamphen, Eastern Rosella, Kaka, Scarlet Robin, Superb Fairy-wren, or Golden Whistler may be noticed first. Only later comes the desire to identify *all* the birds seen on a walk in the bush, or on the seashore. Not that there is anything wrong with noticing colour; it's just that it is only one aspect of a bird's appearance.

When face to face with a completely unknown bird, nothing beats a calm study of its colour and its shape—sometimes easier said than done when it is so close that you could almost touch it and you dare not breathe in case you frighten it away.

First visual impressions are important, and become even more so as your experience grows. A fleeting glimpse can be so incomplete. Yet with experience it is possible to identify many species from that momentary awareness of an out-of-focus bird. At first, these fleeting glimpses only add to your confusion, but hang in there, things will get better. How much better will depend entirely on how much time you are prepared to give.

A birdwatcher's ultimate desire should be to have a really good long look at a bird—any bird, but especially one you think you have not seen before. Somewhere between the fleeting glimpse and the good long look lies a great deal of your routine birdwatching. If the bird happens to call, your task of identification is often made much easier. We'll come back to calls and songs shortly. For now, let's concentrate on observation.

Detailed observation

Just as we suggest that you study the component parts of a landscape and divide it mentally into discrete habitats, we recommend that you look at a bird in 'pieces'.

Look systematically at size, general body shape and colour, head markings, bill shape and length, leg length and foot shape (if the feet are visible). Note the stance

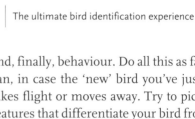

The ultimate bird identification experience

and, finally, behaviour. Do all this as fast as you can, in case the 'new' bird you've just spotted takes flight or moves away. Try to pick out the features that differentiate your bird from all the others. Don't allow yourself to be diverted by the sudden reappearance of another bird you have already identified. Concentrate on the new one.

As soon as possible afterwards, and *before* consulting your field guide, write the details down. You should do it as soon as possible because you cannot hope to hold all the details of a new bird clearly in your mind while you continue your birdwatching (and you may see several new birds on a good day). You should do this *before* consulting your field guide because otherwise you will find that your description changes subtly until it fits one of the birds in the book, and the 'real' bird is lost. The colours in field guides can vary with printing quality and artists' impressions so that no image is a perfect match with what you have seen. Also, there is rarely time to stand with the field guide in your hand and the bird in the bush while you tick off the identification features. Flipping through the illustrations will disturb your concentration and possibly frighten the bird away. Much better to spend the observation time in memorising all the information that you can. Try to keep an open mind.

Write down exactly what you saw (and heard)—no more, no less. This will be a permanent record which you can show to other birdwatchers for positive identification. Add the date, place and time, and any other circumstances that might be useful.

Let's pretend you are looking for the first time at a robin with a pink breast. It is sitting in shadow, and although the pink colour stands out against the tree, you find it hard to judge the exact shade of pink. You're also not quite sure whether the upper parts are black or grey. However, you note that the bird has a white frons (forehead) and that the dark head colour reaches well down below the throat. When the bird moves on, you write these details in your notebook. Later, you reach for your field guide and discover that it was a male of either a Rose or a Pink Robin. You got the top bit right. But did the pink extend right down to the abdomen (Pink Robin)? Did the bird have white tail shafts and a white abdomen (Rose Robin)? These are the necessary *extra* details that you will know to look for next time.

General shape

The body form of many species stands out most distinctly in silhouette. If you are looking at a swan or a cormorant, or a large perching bird such as a lyrebird, then the shape identifies the family almost instantly.

Most small perching birds (the passerines, or songbirds) are more difficult to identify by silhouette as many are rather similar to each other in general shape.

On the other hand, the silhouettes of certain medium-sized passerines such as long slender wattlebirds, fish-tailed drongos and plump-bodied bowerbirds are fairly easy. There are always plenty of exceptions but most shape recognition difficulties lie with the smaller passerines seen against the light. About half of the small Australian honeyeaters have the same generalised silhouette.

Size

The overall size of the bird is important. A scale of relative size, ranging from 'tiny' to 'huge', which you can carry in your mind, is a great tool to use. You might choose to annotate your field guide with the sizes, so that comparisons are readily available.

Size is one of the first points to note as you observe each bird. 'Size of a Silvereye', you think, or 'Size and pointed shape of a starling' (a better thought, because it includes an indication of general shape).

One way to overcome the difficulty in judging size is to choose a set of birds of varying sizes which you can make use of as models or benchmarks, then positively identify every bird you see in relation to your benchmark birds. Our benchmark list is as follows.

OUR BENCHMARK BIRDS

We have selected thirty-two common birds of distinctive (and typical) size, shape and behaviour. Get to know them really well, and make them your permanent models for relative size and shape, for various lighting effects and for flight and other behavioural mannerisms.

Emu huge, ground-dwelling, flightless bird

Stubble Quail small, round-bodied, ground-dwelling quail

Little Penguin medium-sized swimming seabird; the smallest penguin

Sooty Shearwater medium-sized, web-footed, long-winged gliding seabird

Black Swan very large, distinctive, wide-winged, long-necked waterfowl

Pacific Black Duck (Grey Duck NZ) large, solid, typical dabbling duck

Great Cormorant (Black Shag NZ) very large, distinctive, fish-eating cormorant

Great Egret (White Heron NZ) very large, tall, wide-winged, long-legged, slender heron

Swamp Harrier (Australasian Harrier NZ) large, wide-winged, ground-quartering raptor

Australian Hobby and **New Zealand Falcon** medium-sized, slender-winged, fast-flying raptors

Purple Swamphen (Pukeko NZ) large, chunky waterhen

Pied Oystercatcher medium-sized, solid, conspicuous beach wader

Bar-tailed Godwit medium-sized, slender, long-legged, long-billed mudflat wader

Red-necked Stint tiny, compact, typical fast-flying 'flock' wader

Silver Gull and **Red-billed Gull** (NZ) medium-sized, common gulls

Rock Dove (Feral/Domestic/Homing Pigeon) medium-sized, typical fast-flying pigeon

Sulphur-crested Cockatoo large, white, distinctive, raucous, typical cockatoo

Eastern Rosella medium-sized, slender, broad-tailed parrot

Grey Warbler (NZ) tiny, plain, flitting, distinctively calling bush bird

Red Wattlebird medium-sized bird, long slender honeyeater; the second largest honeyeater

Noisy Miner medium-sized, plump-bodied, communal honeyeater

White-plumed Honeyeater small, typical of the bulk of honeyeaters

Grey Fantail (Fantail NZ) small, acrobatic, insectivorous bush bird

Grey Shrike-thrush medium-sized insectivorous bush bird

Black-faced Cuckoo-shrike medium-sized, but slender; wide-ranging conspicuous tree-top forager

Australian Magpie large, aggressive, visible and distinctive omnivore

European Goldfinch small, distinctive finch-like seed-eater

Silvereye tiny, highly mobile, distinctively calling bush bird

Common Blackbird medium-sized, round-bodied, ground-feeding songbird

Common Starling medium-sized ground-feeding bird, 'pointed' in appearance and flight

A suggested rough scale of measurements for grading birds by relative size.

Measurements are of total length from bill tip to tail tip (extremely long tails have been discounted).

Tiny 8–15 cm; small 15–25 cm; medium-sized 25–45 cm; large 45–80 cm; very large 80–150 cm; huge 150–280+ cm.

Posture and activity

Action of wings and legs, type of bill, posture, and attitude when perched, standing, swimming, running or flying — all of these are useful in identification, and many are discussed elsewhere in this book.

It is worth writing down details of a bird's posture and activity that might help you identify it in the future. Making the effort of writing it down ensures remembrance. You are also much more likely to recall your own observations because your memory contains so much extra colour and emotion. Other people's observations may be interesting and instructive, but your own are vivid by comparison because they *are* your own.

Some birds radically change their shape between one behaviour and another. A Great Egret (White Heron; Kotuku) standing alertly at the edge of a swamp is tall, elegant, vertical. The same egret looks horizontal as it peers at tadpoles in the water, or quite dumpy and short as it dozes in the sun with its long neck retracted. In flight, too, egrets and herons bend their necks and change their shape. At first sight, a flying White-faced Heron can be surprisingly difficult for the beginner to identify.

A Magpie Goose is a distinctive goose-like waterbird of 'knob-headed' appearance, easily recognisable as it frequently perches on trees, stumps or posts. Yet in flight it is hump-backed and ponderous, and may be confused with the Australian Pelican at times.

A hunched-up White-headed Pigeon, feathers fluffed out against heavy rain and head sunk back into the shoulders, seems larger than the same bird walking elegantly in the shade under the trees.

Immature birds *sometimes* look 'larger' than their own parents and this, allied to the different plumage stages they may be passing through, can make you think you are looking at a 'new species'!

General colour

General colour is a subjective impression and varies so much with light conditions that it is not always a reliable feature. Before you smile derisively and murmur 'Australian Magpie?' allow us to remind you how many birds are mostly grey, brown or olive. Now double the number, to take in all the young birds that have protective brown colouring. Add the incremental changes in plumage colouring that occur between the colder southern regions and the tropics, and from east to west in Australia. Take account of the variations in island populations. Any of these may be affected by reflections or the quality of light. That said, it is still useful to note down the overall impression of colour that first takes your eye, because in *some* species it is an important diagnostic feature. For birdwatching purposes, 'black' and 'white' are treated as colours.

One example we experience daily is the identification of Brown and Striated Thornbills, which often forage together in our garden. Seen in a poor light they are little brown birds identifiable only by their calls. Most birdwatchers have a group name for small birds which at first sight are brownish to nondescript-looking: 'little brown jobs', or 'LBJs'.

In sunlight the lighter parts of the Striated Thornbill, often the flanks, have a yellowish or yellow-greenish tint, whereas in the Brown Thornbill they are pale buff. This is a useful 'sub-diagnostic' feature—a home-grown one to suit our own local thornbill population when we are looking up into a tall tree and have little hope of seeing the diagnostic face or throat markings as the tiny birds dart about amongst the leaves.

It is important for you to build up your own chart of colour impressions. The above example works for us, but it may not work for you. Obviously we also use calls and behaviour to confirm identity. Brown Thornbills have a strong rich warble and often forage in low bushes. Striated Thornbills' voices are thin and insect-like. They often hang from the outer leaves of tall trees as they forage for insects. They tend to forage higher in the canopy, but this is by no means a universal rule.

Colour traps for the novice

Don't fall into the trap of assuming that the dorsal patterns (the upper surfaces) of birds are dominant and the underparts are mainly soft greys and browns. Later,

Immature Grey Butcherbird. Hattah Kulkyne National Park,
north-west Victoria

when you take a close look at your field guide and read the descriptions, you will realise this is not always the case. Raptors are seen most often from underneath, but so are many small birds, especially in thick bushland. When perched far above you, the breast pattern and underbelly of owls and cuckoos will become your best clues to identification. The bars on the ventral surface of bronze-cuckoos are a good example.

A bird may have three distinct colour patterns to present to the observer.

First is the side-view, perched in a tree at eye-level or below, in conventional 'field guide' lateral posture. This is the presentation that birdwatchers will often call 'a good view'.

The second is the view of the underside of the bird when it is perched above the viewer. Here you will have to rely on your growing knowledge of the markings of the throat, breast, belly and undertail. Familiarity with calls can be particularly helpful here because it gives you a hint on what to look for.

The third colour pattern is the view of the bird as it turns its back or flies away. Obvious examples are Buff-rumped or Yellow-rumped Thornbills, in which identification depends heavily on precise rump or tail colour. Wing and shoulder colour, revealed only in flight, is important in many ducks, waders, pigeons and doves, parrots and sittellas.

Moulting birds of different ages can trick you with plumage variations. Hawks, gulls and pigeons with sub-terminal dark tail bands can lose these temporarily during moult. Eurasian Coots tend to become tan on the wings before the moult. Male fairy-wrens appear patchy, plain or just 'different'.

Apparent colour on a tail may be long wing feathers or a shadow from the wing. Where tail markings are important, you may need to wait until the bird turns around or flies away to make a positive identification.

For various reasons, birds' plumage may be stained or discoloured. When gathering nectar, Red Wattlebirds and some other honeyeaters collect so much pollen on their heads that they seem to have gold or yellow head markings, generating reports of a 'new species'. In red dust areas, especially along the inland roadsides, white parts may become brown or red, perhaps giving the impression of a rufous patch on the breast and flanks. Little Pied Cormorants, Australian Pelicans, herons, ibis and gulls wading or swimming in water containing iron-producing bacteria, may emerge with rusty stained breasts and flanks, and puzzle observers. And, of course, oil spills or heavy pollution cause not only colour change but health problems.

Fruit-eating doves, like children, sometimes dribble fruit juices down their chests and are stained with pink or purple. Grey Shrike-thrushes foraging in burnt mallee scrub have been seen with charcoal streaks and smudges on the body plumage. Choughs and Apostlebirds that have been working with mud may wear light brown masks over their heads and necks as the mud dries.

Interestingly, some bird species look white and clean in all conditions. By contrast with Australian White Ibis, which are often dirty and discoloured, spoonbills always look clean. And, silver-white Royal Spoonbills always look immaculate compared with the sometimes faintly grubby Yellow-billed.

Where the distribution of several robin species overlaps, identification
of 'little brown jobs' can certainly be difficult. This is a juvenile female
Scarlet Robin. Naracoorte, South Australia

Birds in non-adult plumage are often another trap for beginners, especially as
many of the older field guides rarely show details of immature colouring. There are
often striking differences between 'juveniles' and the 'immatures', which are more
easily recognisable as a young version of the adults. Young Nankeen Night Herons,
with a brown-greenish cast to their streaked and mottled appearance, could be taken
for an entirely different species from their black-capped, rufous-backed parents. A
young Eastern Spinebill is a very attractive, plain dark grey and tan honeyeater.

The richly red-brown colours of juvenile whistlers, and the streaks of robins and woodswallows, are very different from the parents, and can cause observers problems if the youngsters are alone.

JUVENILE AND IMMATURE

Juvenile birds are those covered in the feathers that immediately follow the moult of the baby down (the first moult). This stage may last for only a very short period in some species—for example, the Olive Whistler, in which this plumage is a warm reddish brown.

Immature birds may be at any stage between the first moult and full adult breeding plumage. This period may extend for some years and therefore include quite a few annual moults—albatrosses, Brown Goshawk, Kelp Gull (Black-backed Gull NZ), Satin Bowerbird.

Plumage can also show signs of wear. Many birds slowly wear away the tips of their tails, leaving a ragged, dilapidated edge. The longer the period since the last moult, the untidier the wing tips and tail tips may become. Birds that forage on or close to the ground, or habitually climb tree trunks, often show extreme cases of this. Loss of the black pigment melanin from feathers can lead to fading colours in some species.

Recently fledged Nankeen Night Heron. In addition to showing cryptic camouflage, it retains wisps of natal down.

Little Friarbird, showing the coloured bare skin on the face. A widespread nomadic honeyeater of eastern and northern Australia.

Blue-faced Honeyeater, also with bare facial skin, and disruptive camouflage. Hattah-Kulkyne National Park, north-west Victoria

When someone requesting an identification insists that they cannot find anything like it in their field guide, they may be right if they are using an inadequate field guide, if the bird is in the process of changing to an adult, or if it is in immature plumage. For example, the juvenile and immature green plumage of south-eastern Crimson Rosellas is very variable and *can* last into breeding age (which has led to the myth that 'the green ones are the females'). However, a newly fledged bird observer is more likely to insist that their bird is a rare species or 'isn't in the field guide' because their observation skills aren't fully developed. A very experienced bird-watcher once said that the first rule of birdwatching is: 'Never get separated from your lunch.' We think that the second rule is: 'If you think you have seen a rare species, you probably haven't.'

Parts of a bird

Sooner or later, like learning the basic structure of a language or a series of events in history, one has to face up to learning the broad details of the bits of a bird. This is no different to being conversant with the gears of a motor vehicle, the common flowers in your garden, or the colours of the football teams in your regional competition.

It will help if you remember that all body parts are classified as 'soft' or 'hard'. The bill, eyes and eye colour, other soft skin about the head and face, wattles and combs, and also the bare skin surfaces of protruding legs and feet—all these are known collectively as the 'soft parts'. These features tend to lose some or all of their colour upon death. If you discover a freshly dead bird, write down a summary of the soft part colours *quickly*, so that a record is kept. A colour photo would also make a useful record. The feathers and the whole internal skeleton are known as the 'hard parts'.

You need to know a few of the names for the parts of a bird in order to use a field guide adequately. Also, when birdwatching in a group, you gain some class if you can do better than 'Look, it's gotta blue bit near the sharp end and red stripes under its whatsit!' At the front of some field guides (and all of the best ones) there are one or more diagrams labelled variously 'The Parts of a Bird', 'Topography of a Bird', 'Anatomy of a Bird', and so on. They are not there to bamboozle you, but to add to your birdwatching skills.

To make your learning more enjoyable, we suggest you go out and buy a roasted chicken, to act as a sort of prompting device, and a bottle of champers. Settle down with your chicken on a plate, your champagne at the ready and your bird book beside you—and keep those greasy fingers off the book!

Look for the simple things first. Our chicken is a three-dimensional object, an organism with a cylindrical, streamlined body. It has a broad front end and a narrow back end and a lateral appendage at each corner. The two thin ones towards the front are called wings (or flippers in penguins) and the two stubby little ones at the back are called legs. When clothed in feathers (especially the long primaries and secondaries) and given smooth aerodynamic curves by the coverts (covering feathers), a wing is a thing of power and beauty (except in chickens).

Your typical roast chicken lies on its back (the dorsal surface) with its breast and belly (the ventral surface) in the air. Turn your chicken on to its ventral surface (belly downwards), into a flying position, and you will see that the wings and the legs also have an upper (dorsal) and lower (ventral) surface.

No, don't eat it yet. Face it away from you and look along its back (or dorsal surface) from above and behind. It looks the same on each side of the body; in other words, it is bi-laterally symmetrical, with one wing and one leg on each side. The whole body has a left and a right side. We experienced birdwatchers speak fluently of the right flank, the left breast, the right thigh, the left cheek. Do you see all those little goose-bumps in rows across that golden skin drenched in secret herbs and spices? They are the feather tracts, the places where the body feathers grew before plucking. The distribution of these feather tracts varies somewhat between families and genera of birds.

Just in front of you, at the back, is a fatty, flattish but centrally pointed lump. This is the place where the tail feathers were connected, and the fatty lump, which we shall allow you to disrespectfully call the 'parson's nose', is the gland from which the chicken obtained the oils and waxes necessary to keep its feathers in good order. You are now free to eat the chicken. *Bon appétit!*

Now that you've eaten your chicken, we recommend that you borrow a budgerigar —a live one, from a trusting neighbour or friend—to continue your study of the parts of a bird. Budgerigars are birds of the dry centre of Australia, although they range widely across the continent. They tend to live in large flocks which, after periods of high rainfall, may number in the thousands. In the wild, they are yellow and green. Colours such as blue, yellow and white have been selectively bred into them by aviculturists.

Head

There is an obviously dangerous curvy and pointy thing up the front of the budgerigar, as with all birds. This is its beak or bill, which has upper and lower pieces that we call the upper and lower mandibles. This bit bites. It is made of horny stuff, actually keratin, exactly the same as your hair, toenails and fingernails, and also the beaks of turtles, horses' hooves and the external horns of sheep, goats and cattle.

The shape and size of the beak are important clues to a bird's manner of feeding and therefore to the food it eats. In herons, egrets, bitterns, night herons and the Darter, the long sharp bill becomes a 'catapulted' or 'snap-driven' spear for piercing fish. This is achieved by downward-pulling musculature attached to three elongated bones in the central part of the neck. Look for the 'kink' in the neck of these birds. It is the external, visible evidence of the internal anatomical arrangement that accelerates the strike.

Budgerigars. Adult male at left; adult female at right. Note the cere colours. This is a mated pair. Cooper Creek, central South Australia

Straw-necked Ibis. This lovely photograph shows off the iridescent (reflective) wing plumage, the bare black skin of the head, the specialised bill, and the tuft of thin, spinous creamy feathers at the upper breast which give the bird its name.

Seed eaters tend to have short strong beaks (in parrots there is a hook to aid seed extraction). Nectar feeders usually have a curved beak for reaching into flowers. Kookaburras often make a three-point landing on their beaks, which are strong and dagger-like (as are the beaks of butcherbirds and currawongs).

Diurnal birds of prey such as the Peregrine and Grey Falcons, and the Cape Barren Goose, have a bare, thickened sensitive area around the nostrils at the top of the upper beak called the cere. So do parrots. The male budgerigar's featherless cere is blue and the female's brown. The cere of the cockatoo is concealed by feathers.

Bare coloured skin about the eyes, face, crown and neck occurs on many birds. Some examples are Feral Chicken, Common Pheasant, Feral Turkey, Pied Cormorant, Comb-crested Jacana, Masked Lapwing, Spinifex and Partridge Pigeons, Regent Honeyeater and Common Myna. Southern Cassowary, Yellow and Red Wattlebirds and Kokako have coloured wattles. The whole head of Australian White and Straw-necked Ibis, and the larger friarbirds, is covered in bare black skin.

Frontal head shields are prominent on Takehe, Pukeko, Dusky Moorhen and Eurasian Coot. The Southern Cassowary and Noisy Friarbird also have structures and protrusions, called 'casques', on the crown of the head. These coloured areas are all important clues to identification. The Masked Lapwing (previously called Spur-winged Plover) has a sharp spur on each wing.

The budgerigar, like all birds, has two eyes. They are round, have eyelids, and can open and close and blink. In budgies, as with most birds, there is one eye on each side of the head. In some other species, the eyes are placed more frontally, giving them some extra binocular vision, and this is most pronounced in owls.

There is a thin wisp of grey tissue which occasionally moves to and fro across the eye, not up and down. It does not help in identifying birds, but they all have one. This is a protective device known as the nictitating membrane, particularly important in birds that are predatory, or that dive into water head-first, or fly fast through the air to catch prey. Crocodiles have one; humans do not.

Look at the eyes of the budgie again. See the central dark pupil, and the surrounding coloured iris. This iris is a most important identification feature in many birds and it should be tucked away in your memory as something to keep an eye on (pardon the pun). The colour of the iris often changes with increasing age, so that some idea of the stage of maturity can be assessed. A very few adult male birds have a differently coloured iris from the adult female of the same species. The Black-necked Stork springs to mind: the female has a prominent yellow iris, the male does not.

Other species in which eye (iris) colour differs in males and females are the Hardhead, Galah, and Major Mitchell's Cockatoo.

Wings and tails

Budgies dart with incredible speed and agility amongst old trees in inland Australia, their huge flocks resembling shoals of fast-moving green and yellow fish. Their pointed wings are the key to their fast flight.

Feathered wings typify birds and the few truly flightless species clearly had powerful reasons for allowing their long-term loss. Wing shape varies enormously; one of the pleasures of birdwatching is to watch the variety of ways in which birds make use of their wings.

The large ground-running ratites (Ostrich, Emu, Kiwi) have vestigial wings. Penguins' wings have become stiffened flippers. Birds that do not fly long distances

Female Southern Cassowary, exhibiting brilliance of the bare skin.

and also occupy thick vegetation cover develop a rounder wing shape (pheasants, quail, Pheasant Coucal, lyrebird). Birds that fly and glide long distances usually have long, narrow wings (albatrosses, petrels and shearwaters, frigatebirds). Those species that need to lift quite heavy loads have wider wings relative to their length (Australian Pelican, Osprey, White-bellied Sea-Eagle, Swamp Harrier). Fast-flying birds have slender wings with 'points' (shearwaters, many waders, jaegers, falcons, lorikeets, Double-eyed Fig-Parrot, Swift Parrot, cuckoos, swifts, swallows). Fast flight is often associated in the human mind with falcons, but birds can make mistakes, too. The larger parasitic cuckoos have pointed wings for high-speed flight, and the appearance of speeding cuckoos, often in pursuit of each other, usually generates local bird alarm calls.

The wing feathers are grouped in recognisable patches. The longest and strongest are the primary (flight) feathers. These are at the outer end of the wing. The secondaries are next along the inner wing and closer to the body. Lying over these two sets of feathers is a series of covering feathers, of varying lengths: the coverts. These smooth the contours of the wing in flight. The number of primary and secondary feathers in a bird's wing varies between families and species.

Watch those wings. And equally, watch those tails.

When we consider bird's tails, we just think of feathers, but the real tail of the bird is the complex lump of fatty tissue called the parson's nose. In zoological terms, it is comprised of the bulb of the rectrices, pygostyle and uropygial gland (preen gland). Rectrices is the name for the large tail feathers which, like wing feathers, vary in number according to family and species. The tail feathers are mounted deep in the fatty tissue where various muscles control their use.

In flight, birds' tails can be raised or depressed, closed or spread, and constantly twist and turn in flight to aid balance, steering and speed control. They are also used for propping against trees, to counter-balance a bird perched on a loose wire or a swaying branch, and for signalling and courtship. Interesting things, tails.

Legs and feet

At the back and underneath the budgie are the legs and feet, adorned with toes and nails. Notice that the legs are a bit scaly, which perhaps shows a hint of a distant reptilian past.

Birds' legs and feet are as varied as beaks, as they are adapted to many modes of walking, swimming and feeding. Raptors' hard, sharp nails are referred to as talons. Songbirds' feet have three toes forward and one back. When perched, these lock around the branch and enable the bird to hang on even when asleep. Cockatoos, parrots and cuckoos have two toes forward and two back. Grebes and coots have widened flanges (lobes) on their toes. Species with webbed feet may have webbing between just three toes (Mallard) or all four (cormorant) for better propulsion when swimming.

Your budgie can't help with the rest of your study, so please thank it for its assistance and give it back to its owner.

Female Darter using its preen glands and perching in typical 'drying wings' posture.
Little Black Cormorant alongside. Note the webbed feet of each bird.

Positive identification

For beginners, every positively identified new bird carries the excitement of rarity, stimulating your interest and driving you forward. For the old hands a new bird is just as exciting, and the circumstances of its sighting are vividly remembered for a long time. What do we mean by 'positive identification'?

Let's take the familiar Grey Fantail (New Zealand Fantail) as an example. It's an easy species to recognise, with its tinkling, repetitive call, its flirting fan tail and its aerial acrobatics.

Walking along a track between low bushes, you note the fantail's presence amongst a mixed crowd of thornbills and other small birds. The fantail is the most familiar, so you spend little time on it, as you are more interested in a possible new thornbill you have spotted. In fact it is the dancing, turning flight in the air that has told you 'fantail' and you've hardly given the bird itself a glance.

The most experienced birdwatcher we know has a reputation for seeing more species than anyone else on a walk. The reason is that he looks at every bird as if it were new to him. He ticks off in his mind the features that identify it positively. He notes whether it is male or female, adult or immature, in breeding or non-breeding plumage, and whether there are any signs of moult. At the same time he watches for interesting behaviour and associations with other species, looks for food items and listens for calls.

It's a lot to remember each time you see a bird, but it's very satisfying to be able to incorporate all of these things into a successfully completed observation of a species in the bush. This concentration on detail will lead you to ask ever more questions about plumage and behaviour, and that's what we want you to do.

When you next see a fantail, don't dismiss it as an 'easy tick'. Look at the amount of brown or grey in its feathers to judge its maturity. Is it a smaller, duller, female? If you are birdwatching in New Zealand, are you sure that you are looking at the race most common to your island? Check the proportion of white in the tail. Is it a black morph? Does the white ear spot extend below the eye? Unlike in Australia, the New Zealand Fantail often congregates in large winter flocks. How many 'colleagues' are with the bird you are watching?

Getting help with identification

How much information do you need about a bird before you can correctly identify it from a field guide? Let's put it another way. If you needed help with an identification, how would you describe your bird to another birdwatcher?

We have some (real-life) examples of what *not* to say, because we receive many requests for telephone identification at BOCA.

'A medium-sized bird is sitting outside my window.' 'What colour is it?' 'Grey'. 'What else can you see?' 'Nothing else. I saw it yesterday, too.'

'A bird is hidden in the tree outside my window. It's singing. What is it?'

'I want to report a Western Spinebill.' 'Where do you live?' 'Melbourne.' 'Sorry, that's impossible, they're found only in Western Australia.' 'I know it's definitely in my garden,' retorts the caller, 'because I looked it up in my field guide.'

Patient questioning often elicits enough information to make a positive identification. The questions asked of the caller usually run in the following order (the time factor is missing because we are generally discussing a bird seen in the past twenty-four hours):

1 Where do you live?
2 What was the bird doing when you saw it? Was it feeding? Was it with other birds?
3 What size was it? Compare it to a bird *you* know well.
4 What colour was it?
5 What do *you* think it is?
6 Which field guide are you using?

Immature Crimson Rosella of the south-eastern Australian subspecies.
Wilsons Promontory, Victoria

Let's take the questions in turn.

First, the place. Knowing the geographical position will focus the search. Remember that distribution maps are really useful for determining where a bird is *unlikely* to be seen.

Second, behaviour and associated species. If it's swimming like a duck, quacking like a duck and in company with other ducks, there's a pretty good chance it's a duck.

Third, size. Not as easy as it sounds if the caller is not used to judging size. Also, if they are unused to binoculars, they may describe a species as much bigger than its real size. If pressed for beak shape or leg length, most inexperienced callers admit they didn't notice.

White-plumed and Fuscous Honeyeaters at a pool. A wonderful opportunity
to compare two closely related small honeyeaters.

Fourth, colour description. This tends to be divided into head colour, back and
wings, and underparts. A band of colour through the eye may be noticed if it's
extremely striking.

Fifth, a possible identification. Sometimes the caller has already searched dili-
gently through their field guide and found a bird that looks similar but not quite
right. That makes a good starting point for discussion.

Sixth, the field guide. This provides further clues, as field guides vary in their presentation, and it helps to be talking about the same pictures. If the caller is using an
ancient book (such as Cayley's *What Bird is That?*) we explain the problems of using
it for identification.

If identification is still difficult, we might ask for a drawing, or the caller may offer
a photograph. A simple sketch, showing proportion of head, legs and body, and
colours blocked in where known, can often be more revealing than a verbal description. Photographs are helpful in providing relative size and behavioural clues, especially if the bird is in a group.

Birds that have escaped from aviaries are frequently the subject of identification
queries, and can be tough to identify if they are aviary-bred forms of African or
Asian species.

You may have noticed that this book follows approximately the same sequence as
these questions, moving from general appearance and behaviour, down to the colour
of specific body parts. It is only with experience that observers learn to look for the
small details that make identification certain.

Some of these details will be found on the head. Look at beak, cere, frons (forehead), crown of head, cheek, eye colour, eye ring, eyebrow, ear coverts (just behind the eye) and lores (the bit between beak and eye).

The rest of the dorsal surface can be divided into nape of neck, mantle, back, rump, upper tail coverts and upper tail. Some birds are named according to these dorsal features (Black-naped Tern, Rose-crowned Fruit-Dove, Black-tailed Treecreeper, Chestnut-rumped Thornbill, White-naped Honeyeater, Saddleback, Redpoll).

The ventral surface also carries identification clues in many species. We have chin, throat, breast, belly, flanks and undertail coverts, vent, underside of tail, thighs (legs), feet and nails. And don't forget the underwing surfaces (ducks, albatrosses, petrels, raptors). The Black-bellied Storm-Petrel, Letter-winged Kite, Rufous-throated Honeyeater, White-breasted Robin and Lemon-bellied Flycatcher are five birds named for their ventral surface colouring.

Wing and tail feathers obviously vary, but beginners often forget to look for white outer tail feathers, dark bands at the tail tip, and the coloured rump and wing patches revealed when the bird takes flight. As your bird flies away, don't think 'Damn, it's gone', but continue to stare after it for as long as possible, to catch every last detail.

At first, you *need* to look at every detail of every bird, because you are not only learning about that bird, you are gathering knowledge about *all* birds. As your knowledge grows, you will find that you do not always need to look at every detail. Shape alone tells you that you are looking at a pelican. In penguins the most noticeable feature is the set of markings on the head and about the face and neck. Honeyeaters are the same. In ducks, many seabirds and hawks, it is the underwing pattern that is most important. Beyond that, there are too many exceptions to every rule.

Remember that, if the bird seems impossible to identify, it may be an immature bird or a male in non-breeding plumage, an escaped aviary bird, a hybrid (especially if it is a duck or parrot), a bird with too much white (albinism, culminating in *pink*-eyed pure white birds) or too much black (melanism), or a bird with some other plumage aberration (perhaps an Australian King Parrot with yellow spots and blotches).

In your own region you will soon find your own shortcuts. Using the distribution maps you might find, for instance, that the whistlers you are most likely to see are the Golden, the Olive and the Rufous. No-one could mistake a male Golden Whistler for a Rufous. Your main identification problem will be with the females. The female Golden is pale olive-grey above, with a noticeable pale grey wing stripe, and is a plain pale colour below. The female Rufous has a white throat and a pale buff breast and abdomen, with thin dark streaks over throat and breast. The female Olive Whistler has a plain greyish throat; the male's is faintly scalloped.

CHAPTER FIVE

Light and shade

In Chapter Four we discussed the importance of learning about physical features. But in order to see the birds as clearly as you can in a field guide, the light must be bright and the weather calm. And we all know how rare these conditions are. Wind and rain, dawn and twilight, sunshine and shadow—all have an effect on the birds' behaviour and on our birdwatching success.

Light effects

Dawn and evening light gilds or reddens plumage. Reflection from, or onto, birds may alter their apparent colours. Black ravens and crows flash silver in the desert sunlight. The pale breasts of birds pick up green, red, yellow, blue-grey or darker hues from adjacent water, rock or vegetation. Pale birds under the large leaves of tropical canopies may take on a greenish hue.

If you have spent time looking out into your garden at different times of day and in different seasons, you may have noticed how the appearance of leaves and flowers changes through the day.

Take note of the effect of changing light on the plumage of the birds you see.

Backlighting

Even the most colourful birds can appear black in full sun or shade. You will often find yourself in a position where a previously familiar bird seen against the light, or flying over water on a grey day, seems to have no identifying colour, but is a uniform black or grey. These are occasions when your knowledge of flight patterns and body shapes comes into its own.

You may like to start by familiarising yourself with our thirty-two 'benchmark birds' on pages 55–56. A good way to learn body shapes is to trace them from a field guide or photograph. Some field guides illustrate the typical head-on wing shapes of hovering or gliding raptors. The *shape* of the silhouette is the important thing, not the size. There is no need to draw a lifesize Emu! Also eliminate colour as an identification aid. This will train you to look for subtle differences of head, bill and wing shape, which may go unnoticed if you concentrate on colour alone.

Rose-crowned Fruit-Dove, perfectly camouflaged for fruit-bearing
Australian rainforests. Another plump member of the pigeon family.

The recognition of silhouettes in poor light is extremely important for duck shooters if they are not to break the law (and vital for the survival of protected waterfowl in
the duck season). Familiarity with wing patches and coloured plumage is practically
useless when birds are rising in flight from a silver lake into a grey autumn dawn.

Whatever the weather or light conditions, birds appear to lose colour when seen
against a bright sky. The sun need not be very bright to produce this effect. Standing
in tall forest on a dull day, peering up through branches to where a small bird moves
briskly amongst the leaves, may leave you with nothing but a sense of frustration. In
these conditions you need patience, and the ability to follow the birds quietly through
the trees until you can obtain a better view.

Amongst tall trees with an almost continuous canopy, birdwatching is made more
difficult because of the short 'sky spaces' between the treetops. A bird flying above
the canopy may provide less than half a second for you to catch sight of it, focus your
eyes and your binoculars, and pick out the appropriate identifying features.

An easy example is a flock of Yellow-tailed Black-Cockatoos, approaching from
a distance and wailing to each other as they fly. As they cross the tiny patch of open
sky above you there is plenty of time to *confirm* what you *already* guess from their
characteristic calls.

But if the birds are silent, or appear suddenly in the sky with no warning, you are unlikely to identify them in such a short time unless you are already very familiar with their shape or flight behaviour. Sometimes there is no substitute for experience.

One April afternoon, Ken was driving into Yarra Junction township (near Warburton, in southern Victoria). Travelling at sixty kilometres per hour around a right-hand bend he saw a large, loose flock of birds fly overhead at a height of at least sixty metres. They were quickly out of sight to the south. Not a trace of colour could be seen on the birds, which were in silhouette against white cumulus cloud. Ken had to rely on flight mannerisms such as speed of flight, flock spacing and prior knowledge of the shapes, wing beats and relative sizes.

Elimination and realisation took only a fraction of a second. Not Yellow-tailed Black-Cockatoos, not Australian or Little Ravens or Pied Currawongs (the observed birds were too small; their flight style was wrong). Not Red Wattlebirds (these birds were too 'dumpy' and round-tailed and tails not long enough; spacing of individuals in the flock wrong). Not Gang-gang Cockatoos (wing stroke and body proportion completely different); not Common Starlings (these were 'rounder', larger than Starlings could ever be). Not a flock of Rock Doves (domestic pigeons).

They were Satin Bowerbirds, thirty or so, a winter flock heading south to the forested ranges beyond.

In poor light conditions you will achieve better results as you familiarise yourself with the relative sizes of species with similar shapes (and, please believe us, birds *rarely* adopt exactly the same attitudes in trees as that depicted on the pages of the field guides).

BIRD SILHOUETTES

Make some good-sized silhouettes of birds, bats and other flying creatures. Trace them in profile from books (carefully, without damaging the book). Fill the outlines entirely in black and stick them to cards or sheets of heavy paper. Write the correct species on the back of the card. Test yourself every week or so, perhaps adding a few each time.

Gather some fellow birdwatchers around and seat them a few metres away. Hold up a series of silhouettes, first obvious ones such as Emu, Kiwi, Black Swan, Takehe, Pelican, Swallow, then harder ones such as ducks, waders, raptors, flying fox, parrots or bush birds.

If your audience is already fairly skilled in bird recognition, mix the families up.

This is an excellent way to study bird families and species recognition, and it can be adapted for use at schools and to introduce young birdwatchers to the common birds of their region.

Let's say that you have been concentrating for some time on your own regional 'benchmark birds' and you can now confidently relate newly identified birds to your chosen list of species. You will find that because you are so familiar with their size, shape and typical behaviour, you can easily identify them even in silhouette, and silhouette recognition is a vital ingredient of birdwatching whenever the light conditions are poor.

Silhouette: Spotted Turtle-Dove.
Mitcham, Victoria

Silhouette: Purple Swamphen.
Jells Park, Melbourne

In the field you will learn to recognise the raking glides of an albatross, the near-vertical dive of a gannet, the graceful shape of a hovering Black-shouldered Kite, the gait of running water-hens or coots, the zigzag of a fantail, the 'rowing' flight of corvids, and the darting flight of swallows. Flickering, shallow wing-tip beats betray the identity of swifts, or an Australian Hobby moving at speed.

Sun and shade

Whenever possible, stand in the shade with your back to the sun, and look towards the birds you want to observe. This will give you the clearest view, and will also ensure that none of the sun's reflections snoop into your eyes around the edge of binoculars or under your hat.

If the weather is brightly sunny, *don't* look around to see where the sun is. Your sight will be affected for the next two or three minutes and you may lose your bird altogether. Look down at the shadows on the ground and walk into the densest patch you can see. Position yourself with the shadow of your head precisely at the densest part of the tree shadow. In that way, you should have maximum eye comfort and be able to focus in any direction.

Depending on the season, early morning light is low from south-east to north-east, and late afternoon and evening light is low from north-west to south-west. One's instinct is to turn away from the sun and to birdwatch 'down light'.

Little Corellas, golden in the morning light. Marryat Creek, South Australia

At noon, the overhead sun throws light evenly in all directions, so in theory you should be able to see birds equally well in all directions, providing you are looking outward, and not up towards the sun. In the Southern Hemisphere, there is almost always a small slew to the angle of the light even at noon, because in midsummer the sun is as far south as it will ever be, over the Tropic of Capricorn, and then only for a relatively short time. In midwinter it is further away from us to the north, towards and over the Tropic of Cancer. Thus, any birdwatcher operating south of the Tropic of Capricorn will be aware that the noonday sun is still not absolutely overhead, bright and hot though the light may be. So the best view around noon will actually be southwards, for the sun will still be a little behind you.

If you set out on a birdwatching trip in a direction that compels you to shade your eyes all day, from the sunshine or from indirect glaring reflections, your enjoyment of the day will be considerably lessened, if not spoiled altogether.

We recommend that you plan your birdwatching so that, broadly speaking, the light is behind you. Birdwatch by travelling west in the morning (say daylight to about 11 a.m.), making a slight deviation to the south about midday (11 a.m. to 2 p.m.), and then turning east in the afternoon (2 p.m. to sunset and on into the dusk) before returning to your starting point.

VIEWING EXERCISE

Stand in the noon sun, then stand in the shade.

In each position, turn very slowly in a circle, birdwatching as you go. You will notice that the amount of direct sunlight falling on you from above and getting into your eyes around the binoculars influences what colours you see on a bird and also the degree of effort needed to see, interpret and finally to identify the bird.

The best position for birdwatching will soon become obvious to you.

Even on a short walk, it is worth planning your route so that you use the light to your best advantage. If you know that a certain patch will contain a lot of birds, for instance, it is worth taking a longer walk in order to approach it with the sun behind you. Then you will have the best chance of seeing the birds before your presence moves them on.

Camouflage

In general terms, any bird's plumage will provide a certain amount of camouflage in its normal habitat. We see so many bird species on lawns or in open farmland that we may forget that these are not usually their natural environment.

And we need to realise that size has little to do with camouflage. An Emu, feeding quietly with head down along the edge of mallee scrub, resembles a pile of dead vegetation. Think of a group of Brolgas, partly hidden by tall grasses, feeding amongst grey-trunked eucalypts in a swamp. Bush Stone-curlews are almost invisible amongst the litter of a dry woodland. So are nightjars amongst dead leaves. Watch

Galah and Yellow Rosella, drinking. Ripple reflections.
Hattah National Park, Victoria

Glossy Black-Cockatoos slowly moving along the branches of casuarinas, frequently in the shade, their bright red tail-feathers hidden from view. As they feed on the cones they may call softly to each other, and this, and the crack of splitting seed cones, will offer you your best chance of locating them. White corellas, flying high in a clouded blue sky, can be difficult to locate despite their calls. White Terns over tropical islands are almost translucent against the sun . . .

Many species have dark, strongly marked dorsal plumage (merging with the ground if viewed from above) and lighter ventral plumage (merging with patches of sky when viewed from below). Small bush birds are marked in this way for protection against raptors and other predators and, of course, fledglings and immature birds frequently have cryptic colouring so that they blend with the ground, with grasses, and with nests, twigs and branches.

Even a superficial study of a few pages in your field guide will provide examples of species whose colouring blends with their habitat—and some surprising exceptions. Grassland species are often streaked and striated in tints of brown and grey, and this includes emu-wrens, grasswrens, cisticolas and Fernbirds. So you might wonder how male fairy-wrens survive with such bright colours.

Treecreepers, sittellas and Brown Creepers harmonise well with their various habitats of trunks, branches, and ground litter. But male robins often stand out like bright jewels against dark trees and bare branches.

The dominant colour of a bird's plumage, even if brightly coloured, frequently blends with its normal background environment (lorikeets in tropical green leaves, Spinifex Pigeons amongst reddish rocks). In addition, there are often horizontal or vertical marks on the face which divert attention from the round and conspicuous eye, so that as long as the bird remains still, it is 'hidden' from view.

The really difficult birds to locate are, first, those that rely on cryptic colouring plus stillness for concealment, such as quail, many ducklings, button-quail, night herons, stone-curlews; juvenile plovers, lapwings, gulls and terns; frogmouths and nightjars; also quail-thrushes, scrub-robins and Bassian and Russet-tailed Thrushes.

Second are species that frequent dense vegetation and rarely emerge into the open except in darkness, such as some crakes and rails, night herons and bitterns. Birdwatchers describe some of these species as skulking or secretive; rather pejorative words that we think indicates their level of frustration and frequent lack of success in getting a good view of these traditionally hard-to-see birds.

Some bitterns, when disturbed in reeds or bullrushes, adopt a vertical, 'beak in the air' posture which they maintain for some time. Laughing Kookaburras sometimes adopt a similar 'stick posture' when frightened by something overhead which they interpret as threatening. They hold their head and beak vertically, pointing towards the perceived danger, and freeze for several minutes at a time. They have been known to react in this way to aircraft, but the usual cause is a large bird such as a goshawk or a currawong.

There are, of course, many birds that use stillness alone to evade detection, and this may or may not be accompanied by a special behaviour. You may see a large flock of small birds feeding in a patch of trees yet if one bird sounds an alarm, silence falls and it seems as if the tree is empty. Each bird has retired to the nearest shelter (perhaps as small as a gumleaf) and will remain silent and still until it believes that the danger is past.

PART THREE:

Bird behaviour

Male Turquoise Parrot drinking, its colours perfectly
reflected in the water. Chiltern, Victoria

Adult male Chestnut Quail-thrush, beak open, singing.
Wyperfeld National Park, north-west Victoria

CHAPTER SIX

Sound

'Birdwatching' is something of a misnomer, since identification and appreciation of birds is based as much on sound as it is on sight.

Generally speaking, the more primitive the bird, the smaller the range of sounds it will produce. Ratites such as the Emu, Southern Cassowary and Kiwi do not have a wide vocal range. They use thuds, grunts, boomings and whistles to communicate. At the other end of the scale, many songbirds have quite a wide repertoire, using songs, calls, or even mimicry for a number of different purposes.

When looking up the literature, you are unlikely to find 'birdsong', 'bird calls' and the like (even 'communication') listed as the key words—try 'vocalisations' instead. This is perhaps an odd categorisation, since birds have no vocal cords as such; the throat structure that produces sound is called a syrinx.

What is the difference between songs and calls? The convention is that calls are short vocalisations that may be produced by either sex at any time. They are the short 'sentences' of everyday communication: 'Look out!', 'Come and see what I've got', 'Where are you?', 'Get off my tree!' Songs are the long complex phrases sung by males during the breeding season: the avian equivalent of 'Love me tender'.

Many birds learn their vocalisation from others and, before the breeding season begins, may be heard practising quietly to themselves in 'subsong'. Subsong may contain some mimicry of other birds.

The art of listening

It is possible to walk through a landscape not really watching birds at all, yet finishing with a list of twenty bird species identified from calls alone. You need not have seen a single bird. A snatch of song, part-heard, can be just as important as that first, fleeting glimpse. An apparently unusual sound will suddenly trigger your memory.

Stand or sit quietly in one place, head down, eyes closed. Place all your listening faculties on full alert. Listen for bird calls at different levels of sound, from loud to very soft. Be consciously systematic and listen for bird calls from different angles, different heights, and of varying sound quality and volume (intensity). Some of the strong, close calls will drown out distant or softer ones. You may have to listen for the far-off bird to repeat its song. (Zoë's law of birdsong: 'The bird stops calling as soon as you try to draw another observer's attention to it!') Try to categorise the calls, just as you might categorise the size of birds. You might choose to list them according to intensity, position, or meaning (if you can guess at it).

Listen for deep, strong calls: herons, gulls, Wonga Pigeon, cockatoos, Koel, kookaburra, lyrebirds, ravens. Listen for intermediate strength calls: rosellas, wattlebirds and friarbirds, orioles, magpies, Clamorous Reed-Warbler, Common Blackbird. Listen for high-pitched thin calls: fairy-wrens, grasswrens and emu-wrens, gerygones and thornbills, small honeyeaters, flycatchers, swallows, silver-eyes. Listen for bell-like calls: Crimson Rosella, Spotted Pardalote, Crested Bellbird, Bell Miner, Bellbird (NZ).

In your mind, sort all the calls you hear into categories. This will help to remember them. These can be fleeting, wispy little sounds that are barely audible, or sounds that are variously repetitious, staccato, shrill, booming, or panic driven. They may be the sounds of display and courtship, of argument and fighting, of hawk-alarm, or soft comfortable 'at home' sorts of calls: an Olive-backed Oriole, Pied Butcherbird, Common Blackbird or Song Thrush perched, softly singing to itself. (These are the subsongs we mentioned earlier.)

Adult male Magpie-lark at Ormiston Gorge, Northern Territory.
Best-known example of antiphonal duetting.

Pair of Australian Magpies singing. Black-backed subspecies.
Wyperfeld National Park, Victoria

Call descriptions

Two people hearing the same bird call at the same time may later describe it in completely different ways. The human ability to hear very high or low frequency sounds is so variable that where one person hears three notes another may hear five.

Written phonetic representations of bird calls have been around for a long time, many of them using the 'spoken word'. Yet, as we all know, birds do not 'speak'; most of their calls have a whistle-like component. For example, the Willie Wagtail is supposed to sing (whistle) a song resembling the words 'sweet pretty creature'. When faced with such a description in a bird book, read the words offered, look at any help given in the way of spacing of phrases or sounds, then try to *speak* the words given, as you *simultaneously* try to whistle or make a swishing sound to match them. Thus 'sweet pretty creature' becomes a sort of 'shweet pwitty quweettya', much closer to the bird's song. By contrast, the old description of a Restless Flycatcher's 'scissors-grinder' call is not helpful to those of us who have never heard such a sound. You may find it more helpful to invent your own phrases.

You may become very familiar with your local sounds yet have trouble recognising the same species when travelling. This is because birds sometimes have regional 'dialects'.

Although some bird species have supposedly been named for their calls, the informal rather than the standard name may be more appropriate. The Common Koel, that irritating bird which calls for hours from the shadows, is also called the 'wurra-wurra-bird', and the words are beautifully descriptive of the sound. On the other hand, some calls of the currawongs are true to their name.

Written descriptions are not always related directly to the calls; rather, they mimic the rhythmic pattern of the sentence, and here your own regional accent will affect your interpretation. We think the answer is to make up your *own* mnemonics for bird calls. Then you can allow for the notes you hear yourself, and the effort of creating the mnemonic will help you to remember it.

But a word of warning. *Never* assume that the call you can hear is coming from the bird you can see unless you have previously identified it to your satisfaction, or you are accompanied by an experienced birdwatcher who identifies it for you, or you can see the bird's beak and throat moving as it sings. There are some pretty tricky ventriloquists in the bush.

Some mated pairs sing together in such a way that their duet sounds like the song of a single bird. The territorial 'song' of the Magpie-lark is an example of antiphonal duet, in which each bird contributes alternately. Chirruping Wedgebills also call antiphonally to create a continuing 'song' but this may not be limited to a mated pair. The male Eastern Whipbird's 'whip' call is so closely followed by the female's 'crack' response that it sounds like one bird, but if you are close enough to see as well as hear the male, you will realise that the female does not always finish the call in response, which suggests that it is a contact call, useful in dense undergrowth.

Kookaburras gather in family groups to call in chorus, most often to reinforce their territorial boundaries at dawn and dusk. Their supposed ability to anticipate rain *may* have arisen from their tendency to call whenever the sky darkens.

Calls as indicators of behaviour

When you are birdwatching, listen to the birds to pick up clues to their behaviour. Obviously most calls and songs are directly related to courtship or territory and it is when birds are 'showing the flag' that they may be most easily observed.

Small birds are often hidden in vegetation and can be identified only by sound—unless, like fairy-wrens, emu-wrens, Striated Fieldwren, Clamorous Reed-Warbler, cisticolas and others, they move to the top of the plants to proclaim their territory.

Clamorous Reed-Warbler. Plain brown songbirds often have strong, melodious voices. Nelson, western Victoria

The pumping shrieks of the Weka are a feature of New Zealand
wetlands and some forests.

Most rails, swamphens and native-hens, including the Pukeko and Weka, are
extremely noisy, some braying almost like donkeys, but the observer cannot always
find a logical reason for their calls. The Masked Lapwing has a raucous cackling
call that can be heard more than a kilometre away. It is frequently heard at
night. Sulphur-crested Cockatoos scream harshly to each other as they fly. Groups
of Crimson or Eastern Rosellas fighting and squawking will also quickly attract
your attention.

Some birds seem almost to reprimand you for disturbing them. The alarm call
of the White-browed Scrubwren scolds you from the undergrowth. The Willie
Wagtail rattles harshly in unmistakable annoyance, and the Common Blackbird
flies away, screeching alarm. Double-barred Finches erupt from the undergrowth,
calling plaintively.

These reactions to intrusion are different from the aggressive sounds that birds
make as they attack each other in a territorial dispute. A Pallid Cuckoo chasing
another through trees has a series of piercing, rising whistles quite different from
its usual rising scale. If you can recognise it, it will attract your attention and tell
you what to look for.

Alarm or panic calls alert all birds in the vicinity to the arrival of a hawk or some other avian predator. Birds in a local community recognise each other's alarm calls and some respond by flying swiftly away, shrieking their own alarm. Small birds tend to become silent and hide. So, if you hear a potential hawk alarm, look up. Don't linger. A bird of prey can cross a piece of landscape very quickly if it has a mind to. Stop all other activities (even lunch), and run to a place from which you can sweep as much of the adjacent sky as possible. This will increase your chances of spotting the raptor.

Calls of raptors

The cackling, chattering calls of courting or fighting diurnal raptors are sounds to listen for. Calls can be between members of a mated pair, or may be a squabble between species in dispute at a feeding location. Raptors, in spite of their macho image, often have fairly high-pitched, cackling voices.

Flock contact calls

High-flying daytime flocks of corellas, lorikeets, or fig-parrots are very noisy. Some of the *Neophema* parrots, especially the Blue-winged, can be readily heard when flying at height.

The flock contact calls of Rainbow Bee-eaters, some small honeyeaters, wood-swallows, crows and ravens, as well as Silvereyes, are sounds to listen for.

Young birds begging for food

The calls of hungry youngsters can be very persistent and, if the birds live beside your house, downright wearisome. Sometimes you might feel like going out with a spoon and stuffing their beak full of baked beans or plum pudding, just to shut them up!

Nestlings in a songbird's nest may quietly beg from time to time, but this will become an intense burst of sound each time a parent arrives with food. In this way you can time the frequency and duration of feeding, if you happen to be interested in doing so.

Begging on the move

Persistent begging sounds that seem to move about the landscape indicate that one or more young birds are fully mobile, and therefore fledged, and are following their parents about to beg for food. The adults of some parrots (most cockatoos, rosellas, King-Parrots), the larger honeyeaters like wattlebirds, friarbirds and miners, and the Australian Magpie are good examples. The sound of young magpies plaintively begging is a common summer sound.

A young Koel, the 'wurra-wurra-bird', one of the larger parasitic cuckoos, spends a
hot day in a fig tree. The cream crown distinguishes it as an immature bird. The rather
similar adult female would have a black crown and moustachial stripe, and be darker on
the back. The series of streaks, and the spots (ocellations; ocellated plumage) probably
gives camouflage amongst long shadows from stems and also in dappled shade from
leaves. (Look in your field guides at the plumage of the Marbled and Papuan Frogmouths
and compare them with this Koel.) Magnetic Island, Queensland

Morning and evening chorus

We believe that birds call in the morning to let the world know they are still there
and are in control of their territories, and to alert mates or offspring as to their individual position.

Why don't you set the alarm clock and wake up before 'dawn's first light'? Position
yourself suitably and listen for the first bird call of the morning. Write down what it
is and also the time. Then add others sequentially as they call. Try to record unknown
species' calls as well. Do it by description in words or a sketch of the way the sounds
seem to be. You will have to identify these birds later. Build your list for (say) one
hour. Once daylight has fully arrived, the nature of the songs and calls should dimin-
ish, or gradually become 'daily routine calls'.

Do this on and off over several months; a calendar year if you have the endurance.
Graph your results and you should have a very clear picture of how and when your
local group of birds welcomes each day. You will soon see that time patterns sometimes alter on very windy mornings, on overcast mornings (which may include heavy
rain at dawn), or during any unusual extremes of temperature.

Evening choruses tend to be more diffuse, a little less predictable, and prevailing temperature and weather conditions will affect the end product. But certainly repeat the morning exercise in the evenings if you can. Sitting quietly in a forest, on a river-bank, at a farm dam or an inland stock tank, or on the porch of a house will be an interesting and restful experience. Take the insect repellent and a jacket.

If you watch and listen in your own garden you may find that, during the breeding months certain birds sing from the same perch each evening just before dark. Well-known examples are kookaburra and Common Blackbird.

Ventriloquial calls

Sometimes a sound appears to originate some distance from the calling bird. These calls are known as ventriloquial calls. Most cuckoos, the Western and Eastern Yellow Robins, the Crested Bellbird, both wedgebills and the Rufous Songlark seem to be able to fool their hearers in this way. Undoubtedly there are others.

It is possible to stand in front of a calling Fan-tailed Cuckoo and barely hear its call if its head is turned away. Once it faces you, the sound is very powerful. The cuckoo seems to give highly directed calls, and the effect is also ventriloquial. If you do not have the bird in sight you may take a while to locate it and you feel pretty good when you do (or a little foolish if it is sitting only metres above you!).

In forested country, or in rocky gorges, echoes will affect what you hear.

Mimicry

A number of bird species specialise in reproducing the songs of other species that live about them. Different species do it for different purposes.

Superb and Albert's Lyrebirds, and many bower-birds, incorporate mimicry into display rituals. Some larger honeyeaters mimic each other's calls at feeding locations, perhaps to escape competitive attention if the bird doing the mimicry is outnumbered by another species. A Regent Honeyeater was recently described mimicking the calls of friarbirds. Other species use mimicry when perched quietly somewhere. Sometimes it is very clear, at other times barely audible, a subsong. Mimicking species include the Olive-backed Oriole, Grey and Pied Butcherbirds, Mistletoebird, Common Starling and Common Myna.

Bark-foraging Crested Shrike-tit in typical pose. The black chin indicates a male.

Nocturnal calls

Many bird species travel at night. You can easily identify the louder passing bird traffic, such as Masked Lapwings, late at night while in bed or watching Test cricket.

Kiwis are about at night, of course, and frequently call, but are flightless. Some birds fly, calling, in late evening or at night. Examples are Black Swans, some ducks, Dusky Moorhens, Eurasian Coots, Masked and Banded Lapwings.

Penguins, shearwaters and some petrels are very noisy at night, at colonies and breeding burrows. Crakes, rails and other members of the Rallidae family make their pumping shrieks, which can carry for long distances. Some waders and gulls are about at night, calling. The few remaining male Kakapo, another flightless species, enter a nocturnal booming period that lasts nightly for several months as they gather to display in island refuges in southern New Zealand.

Night-time repetitive calls of the Pallid Cuckoo and Common Koel have been placed in the 'brain fever bird' category by hapless non-sleepers in hot climates. Most owls, nightjars and the Australian Owlet-nightjar call at night, but certainly not every night, and are far more likely to be heard in their breeding seasons.

Occasionally lyrebirds give brief nocturnal performances, and the Willie Wagtail, on clear warm nights in spring and summer, may be heard giving territorial calls. Magpies are known to sing in the moonlight.

Other sounds to listen for

Some birds betray themselves by sounds other than calls and a quick glance is all that is needed to confirm their identity.

The sound of wings
Most doves and pigeons that feed on the ground rise abruptly with a clatter of wings at the slightest disturbance, and familiarity with their dorsal colour patterns will help you to identify them as they fly away. Eastern Spinebills dart above your head with a loud 'flick' of their wings, then show bright white outer tail-feathers against their dark bodies as they dive into cover. Chapter Eight, 'Flight', describes many other birds that make wing noises.

Scrabbling in bark
Tree-creepers, some honeyeaters, sittellas, Crested Shrike-tit, Grey and Little Shrike-thrushes, Grey (and sometimes Pied) Currawong and White-winged Choughs are amongst species that consistently scrabble about on tree trunks, searching bark snared in forks, flicking flakes off the trunks and larger branches and even swinging from loose bark strands in their search for invertebrates.

Chewing sounds
Galahs and Sulphur-crested Cockatoos are sometimes betrayed by splintering noises as they chew around the edges of nest hollows in trees. If you are really unlucky, or if

you have established a bird feeder for parrots and cockatoos but failed to replenish it, the sound will be your fast-crumbling balcony rail, fascia boards or red cedar window and door frames. Sometimes these birds excavate putty from around glazing. They will fill in any idle time by gently and methodically destroying your house and most of the nearer garden trees as well. Keas, in similar vein, do their collective best to demolish parked vehicles, tents and rucksacks in the Southern Alps of New Zealand.

Loud eating noises
Red-tailed and Glossy Black-Cockatoos can be audibly detected opening woody fruits and cones as they feed. Rosellas and pardalotes cracking galls on leaves can make quite a noise. One wonders whether these birds are eating with their beaks open . . .

The patter of falling leaves and buds
Various fruit-doves, Gang-gang Cockatoos, lorikeets and rosellas, often sit quietly, dropping a continuous shower of leaves, fruit scraps, branchlets and cones as they feed overhead. In hot weather the patter of falling debris onto dry leaf litter gives away the location of many a parrot.

Birds raking leaf litter
Raking activity provides both visual and audible clues to the presence of birds. Typical examples are Malleefowl, button-quail, lyrebirds, some treecreepers (particularly the Brown), quail-thrushes, some of the robins, babblers, Chowchilla and Logrunner, White-winged Chough and Apostlebird, Common Blackbird and Song Thrush, Bassian and Russet-tailed Thrushes.

   Button-quail make little open saucer-shaped depressions or clearings on the forest floor, and recognition of these is often the first step towards finding these birds. The next step is to find the most recently made saucers. Look ahead, low down, some twenty, thirty or forty metres in front of you, as you quietly move over button-quail feeding saucers. This will offer the best chance of seeing the culprits.

Other environmental sounds

Learn to distinguish between bird calls and the sounds of other creatures. It is important that you try to sort out the sounds of tree crickets, wetas and grasshoppers, the European mole cricket, cicadas, the hum of bees, European wasps and flies, small frogs, mason wasps and gecko barkings and clicks. Some baby bush birds—which make a 'tzzztzzztzzz' sound—could be mistaken for tree crickets. At night, some arboreal marsupial calls and some small bat or flying fox calls may be mistaken for bird calls overhead.

A Yellow-tailed Black-Cockatoo executes a 'textbook' extraction of a wood-boring witchetty grub from an Acacia trunk. The pink skin of the eye indicates a male. Yarran Dheran Reserve, Melbourne

WALK IN A RAINFOREST

Early one January morning we were the first visitors to Mary Cairncross Park in
south-east Queensland, less than a two-hour drive north of Brisbane. (This park
is situated on a high east–west trending ridge overlooking the Glass House Mountains
from the north. It is about forty kilometres due west of Caloundra. If you visit, allow
yourself at least three hours to take full advantage of the birdwatching potential of the
park. From the car park there is a spectacular view towards Brisbane to the south. The
park is a remnant of rainforest, surrounded by open farmland.)

The sky was still overcast and traces of a light overnight fog hung low in the air. There
was barely any breeze. As we moved towards the rainforest entrance, a pair of Australian
Brush-turkeys walked slowly past. On our right a bank of shrubs held several Brown
Cuckoo-Doves sitting quietly on the outer branches.

Suddenly, the thick vegetation closed over us. We were still attuned to a more visual
world, unprepared for the sudden darkness and colder temperature of the forest. Trees
dripped water as the fog condensed on the leaves, and the formed track on the floor of
the forest was quite wet, practically silent to walk on.

Inside a rainforest there are echoes, magnifications. Between bursts of startling sound
it can be eerily silent. Sounds become strong, rounded, liquid—a pleasure to hear.
Distance is hard to judge, as sound reverberates under the canopy. It is quite different to
being in woodland, or scrub, or any other habitat.

Because of the dim light, binoculars were of little use. We had to rely on sound to find,
then identify, many of the birds. Small frogs called here and there, with trills and croaks.
Some deep-throated cooings suggested fruit-doves in the canopy. Every so often,
something would fall to the forest floor with a distinct 'plop'. Fruits, no doubt, but were
they falling naturally?

Not far along the track we became aware of a pile of vegetation. Peering into the
gloom, we resolved it as a nest mound of the Brush-turkey. We heard the shrill shrieks of
Rainbow Lorikeets passing overhead, and the clattering of a Little Friarbird. The sweet
piercing note of a Grey Shrike-thrush, normally very familiar, took on a ventriloquial
quality in the half dark.

Twitterings near the ground heralded a pair of perky, long-legged Yellow-throated
Scrubwrens, the first of many. They travelled at some distance from each other,
constantly twittering and softly 'ticking' to keep contact as they hopped along the track
and into the litter on each side. They became our constant companions and we rapidly
learned to pick out their call from the rest of the sounds. They must surely be amongst
the most attractive of the scrubwren group. We admired the pinkness of their legs and
feet. Moderately tame, they let us come quite close, but sometimes one would suddenly
break into louder, sharper 'tick-tick' scolding and they would then move away rapidly.
Here and there we saw old nests of this species: dark oval bundles of shrivelled plant
material, perhaps rootlets and fern fragments, suspended on a woven strand from tree
limbs. Each had a side entrance hole. Some were still in good repair, others collapsed
and misshapen.

A sharp 'schurr' and then another 'sschurrr' focused our attention sharply ahead. Slow stalking and edging along the path eventually led us to a robin perched first on a guide rail, then on the side of a tree trunk at head height. It was a soft yellow-breasted bird, round-bodied and big-headed, large-eyed like all the robins. Another appeared. They flew away from us together, with a 'prrrp-prrrp' of wings, revealing a plain grey-green back and a narrow wing bar. We waited silently until they returned to feed from low perches near the track, jumping to the ground to grab tiny caterpillars or grubs. At such close quarters we could see a smudge of white just in front of the eye, on the lores. These were Pale Yellow Robins, lovely little birds in the dark jungle.

The small patches of sky above us were turning from grey to yellow as the sun rose higher and the sky cleared. All around us doves or pigeons were calling; but high in the trees, coming from three different directions, were strange mewings, caterwauls, repeated a few times, then dying away. This seemed like a territorial call, because no sooner had it come from one direction than it was promptly repeated from the other two. We used our binoculars and eventually saw a faint flash of something green far above us. It flew, disappeared, reappeared. The calls were something like a very small baby crying in the treetops. More flashes of green. We were stalking it together, craning back, necks almost breaking, each adding tiny fragments of plumage description to the avian jigsaw . . . some pale greenish breast, a green crown. The bird snapped a tiny branch, and flew off with it. The bill was chunky, pale. 'Got it!' 'Green Catbird'. Yes, the calls were cat-like, mewing (but our first description to each other was of a baby crying).

Several times we had heard 'zizz'-ing, chittering calls, something like those of Striated Thornbills, but had seen nothing. Now, quite near to us, a small plain bird clambered around in the swinging vines. In the dim light we could see no distinguishing marks, no real colour patterns. It flew off along the track ahead. What was it?

Once we saw the first, it became easier to see others as we walked. Was this bird's call ventriloquial? We had been consistently looking too high in the trees. Or was it simply the echo effect of the rainforest?

All of a sudden, a scuffle broke out in a sunlit patch of large bright green leaves. Branchlets rattled, there was an outburst of 'wak-wak' sounds. From the centre of the noise erupted two fruit-doves, one chasing the other, huge by comparison with all the small birds we had been watching. The chase stopped as quickly as it had begun, and both vanished. Large as the birds were, the big leaves and strong contrasts of the sub-tropical vegetation provided complete camouflage as long as they sat still.

Then, from a little distance away, one of the birds began to call: a meditative, low, bubbling call, obviously dove-like. The calls were always from the same direction, giving us plenty of time to search every branch and leaf in the canopy around us. And each time we gave up in frustration, it called once again, bringing us back to our starting point.

A friendly man with a small boy came along the track at that point and asked what we were looking for. 'We think there's a Wompoo Fruit-Dove nearby, but the damned thing's too high up in the branches,' we replied.

'You mean that one?' said the small boy. And there it was, two metres above us, resting quietly on a branch. At first we could see only the rich purple throat and breast, brilliant yellow belly and undertail coverts, but by moving along the track we could also see the bright green back and pale head, blending so well with the leaves.

'We come here every week,' said the small boy cheerfully. 'There's often one sitting over there.'

We all stared at the Fruit-Dove for a while (and the bird stared smugly back). Only the delight of adding a new bird to our list overcame our embarrassment at not having been able to see such a large and brightly coloured bird.

We never did lay eyes on the Rose-crowned Fruit-Doves, which must have been feeding on the top of the canopy. We could hear them all morning, giving their characteristic, accelerating calls which, like the call of the Peaceful Dove and the Pheasant Coucal, can be so evocative of the tropics.

Once the sun was high in the sky, birds above us were frequently seen only in silhouette, so we concentrated on the understorey.

In a little sunlit patch of path near a fallen tree, movement and acid-edged calls simultaneously drew our attention. A Rufous Fantail, spectacular in bright rufous with black and white garnishings, put on a great display of running short flights and pirouettes. The little upward flights and brief perchings never took it far; mostly it remained close to the ground. The energetic activity was accompanied by sharp little 'twizz-ing' notes, and occasionally a short trilling song.

And nearby, there was another of those plain brown small birds—a 'little brown job' if ever there was one. By now, we had excavated our field guide from the backpack. Faintly upturned flat black beak, long pale legs, a wash of soft buffy browns all over, vaguely paler below—we agreed that our personal mystery bird in the park was the Large-billed Scrubwren, a bird we don't encounter often in Victoria.

Persistent new calls came into our consciousness. A triple 'whichy-whichy-whichyoo', quite mellow and rounded, came from above, then over there, then behind us. Something grey and tan was glimpsed in quick, flickering flight. Patience rewarded us with a fleeting look at the whole bird: the Black-faced Monarch.

And all of a sudden, just nearby, two more birds were fronting up to it. Sharply scolding, similar at first sight but subtly different, two Spectacled Monarchs drove the first bird away. But whose calls had we first heard? Later we heard the same calls and we saw another Black-faced Monarch, on its own. Mystery solved.

As we returned, blinking, into the light and heat of a summer morning, Pied Currawongs could be heard giving their ringing double calls across the valley. This was a bird we knew well, easy to identify by sound. The Catbirds called again. A Brown Cuckoo-Dove, long-tailed and drowsy, was sunning itself on a bare branch. Laughing Kookaburras, five of them, were in the car park, and briefly, bunched together in dead twigs atop a large *Acacia*, gave a half-hearted little chorus, never really got it going, and coughed to a stop. The Brush-turkeys were still there, walking slowly amongst the increasing rows of cars. Overhead, a soundless scatter of racing black sickle shapes at height was a flock of White-throated Needletails (Spine-tailed Swifts) feeding above the ridge, disappearing towards a cloudbank to the west. It had become very hot and very humid very quickly. It was time to leave.

CHAPTER SEVEN

Daily routines

Birds have daily routines, just as humans do.

Each morning we wake up, stretch, chat to each other, shower and groom ourselves, eat breakfast, then start on the work of the day, which may vary according to our age and the season. In the middle of the day we have a light meal, then continue with our activities. At night we eat dinner and prepare to sleep.

Birds wake up, usually pre-daylight, and call to announce that they have survived the night, are still in control of their territory, or want to make contact with other birds. They may preen their own feathers and perhaps those of their partners, and eventually set off to catch the proverbial local worm or fly to a feeding ground. They tend to relax a bit in the middle of the day, may quarter their territory, find more food in the late afternoon and evening, drink, perhaps preen, and go to roost.

Generally, the best times to watch birds are early to mid morning and late afternoon, especially in hot weather. An excellent time for birdwatching is when the sun comes out after a shower of rain. The warmth and moisture bring out birds and insects together.

If you regularly birdwatch in the same place but at varying times, you will probably find that the greatest activity occurs at roughly the same time each day unless the weather is very unusual. In our own valley we can rely on a certain amount of movement soon after dawn, a great swell of activity between ten and eleven in the morning, and another swell an hour or so before dark. An exception to this is when the various eucalypts come into bloom. During autumn, for example, our Swamp Gums are filled with Red Wattlebirds from dawn to dusk.

People who keep yearly records find that seasonal arrivals and departures can be predicted quite accurately, and they may be able to 'forecast' an unusually dry or wet season according to the birds' movements.

In temperate climates

Because southern Australasian summer nights and early mornings are often cold or cool, aerial insect activity is slow to begin. Invertebrates may take a considerable time after daybreak to get moving.

In south-eastern Australia, small numbers of White-throated Needletails may roost in the tree foliage in the forested ranges on some summer nights. These swifts do not spring out of bed at daybreak, but seem to wait for a while—perhaps half an hour or so—before appearing in flight low in the valleys and across the hilltops. They feed fairly close to the treetops for a while, gradually rising as their aerial prey also begins its daily ascent.

In tropical climates

In the tropics, bird behaviour can be very different. Observers of hot-climate birds should be out *before* daylight to get the best of the couple of hours following sun-up. The heat takes over after that and bird activity can become markedly subdued.

One January morning in 1996 we were birding at daybreak in south-east Queensland. We walked along a narrow road in a well-vegetated gully below ridges capped by Bunya Pines. We had a wonderful two hours from about 5 a.m. to 7 a.m. and saw many interesting species.

But at about 7.15 a.m. the heat increased noticeably as the sun rose above the ridge, and at precisely 7.30 a.m. an amazing wall of sound rose up to surround us. Hundreds of cicadas burst into song at once and, as they did so, bird activity dropped right away. Our birdwatching abruptly ceased. The bird calls (on which we had relied in the dense rainforest) were drowned by the cacophony from the insects. The contrast between the early bird activity in the morning's coolness and the sudden onslaught of hot sun and cicada noise was stunning.

All in the same few minutes, the little valley filled with hundreds of butterflies of several species, some pitching on the moist earth to drink, but most moving steadily northwards within three metres of the ground. It was a breathtaking sight. We stood amongst the butterflies for an hour, then went back to breakfast. Insects rule, okay?

Tidal routines

If you cannot watch birds early in the day, then a visit to a wetland or the seashore later in the day is the best option, because there will usually be some activity there. On your way you may see a few raptors gliding in circles. The best lift into the sky comes later in the day, as the air warms and begins to rise in columns (convection cells) spaced out across the countryside.

The group of birds broadly called waders includes many annual migrants, which tend to gather on suitable sands and mudbanks or flats between high tides to feed. As soon as the tide turns and begins to ebb, the waders move on to the increasingly exposed surfaces, which they search for food. As the tide falls, the birds tend to move further and further away from the shoreline. Birds that could at first be readily identified at fairly short range now require good field glasses or the trusty telescope. Many other species may join in: Black Swans, various ducks, herons and egrets, ibis, gulls, even ravens and Common Starlings.

Australian Pelican preening. Jells Park, Melbourne

As the low tide turns again to creep over the ground, so the waders are slowly herded back towards the shore. Eventually, they break off feeding and fly to a nearby secure high spot to roost in a large huddle and await the beginning of the ebb flow once more. Huddled, roosting waders should not be disturbed needlessly, as their life is dictated more by the tides than by daylight, and this is their time of rest.

Birdwatchers need to attune themselves to the local tidal sequence and range before setting out to watch coastal waders. Tide tables are published for most major localities. If you don't plan ahead, your wader-watch may be a failure.

Feeding

The size of a bird is not necessarily a guide to the size of its food. You may receive more clues on feeding behaviour from the size and shape of beaks and feet than from bodies.

Birds feed in virtually every habitat on earth. Knowledge of the foods they seek, and the feeding strategies they employ, will help you to find and identify them. Many of the family behaviours we have previously described are connected with foraging for food.

Few species are limited to a single food item for survival, but birds will certainly show food preferences—ignoring some berries, for instance, until they have no choice but to eat them. Obviously some foods *taste* better. Different food preferences and hence feeding strategies in closely related species allow them to co-exist within a single habitat.

The parents of most specialist seed eaters, fruit eaters and honeyeaters provide protein-rich invertebrate food to their nestlings and fledglings, eventually 'weaning' them onto the adult foods.

Gang-gangs feeding quietly in the crown of a heavily fruiting eucalypt may, by the end of the day, create a thick carpet of green leaves, twigs and crushed gumnuts on the ground under the tree. Parrots and cockatoos are usually very wasteful feeders. Glossy Black-Cockatoos are an example of a large cockatoo that feeds on tiny seeds.

Major Mitchell's Cockatoo feeding on seeds of paddy melons.
Mungo National Park, southern New South Wales

They have to spend many hours each day extracting the seeds from the cones of casuarina trees and recent studies have shown that they choose to feed in trees with a high nutritional content in the seed. This nutritional value depends largely on the soil in which the trees grow. Replacement of one patch of felled casuarinas with another stand planted in the district may be no fair exchange at all. From the viewpoint of a Glossy, seeds ain't always seeds.

Neither Australia nor New Zealand has any woodpeckers (family Picidae), probably the best-known example of birds that extract insects from tree trunks and branches. Today this role is filled largely by certain black-cockatoos, parrots and riflebirds in Australia, and by the Kaka in New Zealand. Black-cockatoos can leave grub-extraction scars that may last for years. Any such scar in a grove of trees means that, eventually, the cockatoos are likely to return and rework the trees in the area.

Riflebirds work rotting wood and bark in tropical wet rainforests, ripping older boughs to pieces in a search for insects and their larvae. Tearing and scratching sounds are commonly heard where these birds are at work.

HUIA

The recently extinct Huia in New Zealand was also a tearer of rotting wood. The lovely paintings that have been prepared from old museum skins show that a pair of these birds, while looking alike in general body plumage, had amazingly varied bill length and shape. The female's bill was long—about 105 mm—down-curved and slender for deep probing of insect burrows. The male had a relatively short bill—about 60 mm—for chiselling use. Each bird of the pair had a precise role in food gathering. The last officially recognised Huia was recorded in 1907, although other reports were made through to 1920.

Some birds have to spend a great deal of their day actively removing their food from its shell, case, pod or cone, digging it out of soil, sand, or stones, or scraping aside the leaves and twigs on the forest floor.

Small-insect eaters do little to prepare their food before their meal, but kookaburras bash their food on a nearby branch to soften it before swallowing it whole. We've seen a kookaburra beating up a sausage from a barbecue, and fledgling kookaburras bashing small sticks 'to death'. This eating technique is the opposite of many rails, birds of prey and corvids (crows and ravens), which secure their food with their feet while they remove vegetable pulp, fur, feathers and flesh, or even plastic wrappers.

Ibis, rails, gulls, Australian Magpie, currawongs, ravens and crows, House Sparrow and Common Myna are examples of species that will try a wide variety of foods and will scavenge around rubbish dumps, schools or fast-food outlets. Ducks and corvids may carry hard food to water to soften it. We know of one raven that unsuccessfully tried to soften cooked chicken bones in this way.

Some small passerines hunt food through most of the daylight hours. Nectar and pollen feeders will visit the same flowers more than once a day. Tidal flows and floods will affect the feeding behaviour of wetland and wading birds whose prey is available only in shallow water.

In past years, knowledge about foods eaten by birds was frequently gained by examining the contents of the gut, which required that the bird be sacrificed. Careful observation and photography, used in tandem, are legitimate and useful methods of gathering information without going to such an extreme. The multiple images obtained on video film or by automatic camera can show the detail of foods and feeding behaviour without harming the birds.

Signs, clues and residues

It is appropriate, in this chapter, to introduce some avian bush detective work: how to read the little signs that tell you that birds have been carrying out their daily routines.

Here is a list of things to look for, many of which will lead you to the birds responsible.

- Pressed tracks and trails or small tunnels in and through grasses, swamps and undergrowth (these are often made by or used by birds).
- Clear bird footprints in a swamp or on a beach.
- Stray moulted feathers, telling you which birds have recently been in the area
- Evidence of predation, or of a natural death in the family, which can be seen occasionally as a pile of feathers, skin scraps or bits of bone.
- Eggshell scraps, which are sometimes dumped by parent birds for the purpose of hygiene and secrecy. (Sometimes a whole egg on the ground suggests that a bird was forced to lay an egg under stress.)
- Abandoned or damaged nests, which will tell you much about the location likely to be chosen for the next nest of that species, and increase your chances of seeing it.
- Little scrapes and scratches on the ground where birds have fed, which may lead you to quail, button-quail, pittas, lyrebirds or thrushes.
- Polished or smoothed surfaces around a tree-spout or a hole in the trunk, which indicate recent use. (Spiders' webs over a dull entrance, perhaps leaf and stick debris behind, indicate a 'cold' hole.)
- A half-circle of penguin, gannet or cormorant whitewash, which will show you which way the wind was blowing recently. (The birds on such surface nests always face the wind.)
- Patches of droppings under tall trees, which may show you the way to an owl or kookaburra roost. (Swallows and martins leave a little pile beneath a nest.)
- Regurgitated pellets packed with hard, furry, scaly, woody and otherwise indigestible bits of prey or food items. (These should be very carefully examined, *and left where they are* for further research in the case of birds of prey and owls.)

Drinking

Birds drink in order to balance the moisture content of their bodies (as we all do) and it follows that birds that eat very dry foods such as seeds may need to drink more

Buff-banded Rail in wing-comfort stretch. The general similarity
to the New Zealand Weka, also a rail, is obvious.

often than those that eat insects, meat, nectar or fruit. Mind you, seed does contain
some moisture.

Larger birds with a crop, such as parrots and doves, *need* to drink only once a day,
but the smaller seed-eating passerines, such as finches, must drink frequently,
especially in hot weather. Although small seed-eaters, such as Budgerigars, can survive for long periods without drinking, they will urgently need to replace moisture if
the temperature rises above thirty degrees Celsius.

Birds obtain water from a variety of sources: groundwater such as streams, lakes
and puddles; dew, house gutters and dripping taps; wet leaves and falling rain.
In arid zones, the distribution of some bird species relates directly to the presence
of water.

Penguins may seek out a freshwater stream after coming ashore from a long
period at sea. Gulls, terns and skuas often do the same. Bronzewings, parrots and
cockatoos may fly long distances each day to reach water.

Most birds take a mouthful of water, then turn their bills up and allow the water to
run down their throats, but doves and shorebirds suck water by muscular movements of the throat. Tongues adapted for sucking nectar can also be used for sucking

water, so the brush tongue of honeyeaters can be used to lap water. Australian Pelicans on eggs and brooding small young at an inland lake sometimes open their bills wide in a sudden shower of rain, to take advantage of the fresh water without leaving their nests. Swifts and swiftlets always drink on the wing, swooping down and touching the lower mandible into the water as they fly across the water surface with a slightly reduced depth to each wing stroke. Swallows often do this too, although it is actually hard to know whether they are drinking or snatching tiny insects from the surface. A good opportunity for some close observation, here.

If you are able to watch a large number of birds coming to drink at a lake or an inland dam, you will see evidence of a hierarchy, or pecking order. Dominant adults will drink first. It has often been said that a group of parrots will leave a lookout in a nearby tree, to warn the drinkers of danger. Is this folklore or is it not?

Coming down to drink in the open, at ground level, makes small birds vulnerable to predation and they will leave at the slightest hint of danger. To watch them you will need to establish some sort of hide or camouflage and keep very still. Sit quietly, watch and record which bird species come to the water, when they come, and what they do when they get there. Next time you see birds drinking, study their method of obtaining water. How does each species go about getting its drink? Which species are dominant? And what happens next?

Every garden needs a water supply to attract birds. Make sure yours is up to scratch.

Bathing

Bathing is an important requirement for most birds. Sooner or later they will want to take a bath, and they seem to enjoy it even in the coldest weather. Some birds 'tip-toe' into the water, bob down briefly and fly to a perch to dry off. Others throw them-selves into the task, vigorously scattering water in all directions. Red Wattlebirds and others make rapid plunges into deep water and are out within seconds. This is called dash-bathing.

If you have a birdbath in your garden, do keep it clean and change the water daily. Birds prefer fresh, clean water (rainwater, not chemically treated, is best of all).

Rain-bathing, foliage-bathing

Many birds take the opportunity to bathe during rain. A thunderstorm or a sudden sharp fall of rain after a dry spell in summer will often trigger fascinating behaviour as birds take advantage of it. Galahs indulge in lovely acrobatics, dangling upside-down from wires or branches, letting their wings flop out to their full extension, twisting and turning their bodies to get the plumage as wet as possible. This is so commonly observed that the terms 'rain-dancing' or 'rain-bathing' have been used to describe it. Once satisfied, the Galahs indulge in long bouts of feather grooming. Ken once observed Black-faced Cuckoo-shrikes doing the same thing, twisting and turn-ing upside-down for a short period in unexpected heavy rain on a hot day.

| Superb Lyrebird bathing. Tara-Bulga National Park, eastern Victoria

Wet foliage, especially if it is fine-leafed and dense, will hold a great deal of water after rain has ceased. On various occasions and at different localities we have observed small flocks of Australian King-Parrots, mixed Rainbow and Musk Lorikeets, Red Wattlebirds, White-browed Woodswallows and (once) a single Olive-backed Oriole throwing themselves into dense wet foliage, almost skidding over the surface of it with tails fanned and wings outstretched (in no way resembling feeding behaviour) and clearly getting just as wet as they possibly could. Preening and shaking of the plumage immediately followed the foliage-bathing activity every time.

Sometimes, after a very heavy dew, we have seen Rainbow Lorikeets, and once, in another location, we saw Little Wattlebirds foliage-bathing in the early morning. Again, the birds were literally throwing themselves into the dense foliage and, once wet, settling down nearby to preen.

ARTIFICIAL RAIN

You can replicate rainfall in your garden, on a hot afternoon in summer, by fixing a fine-spraying nozzle of a garden hose so that it plays lightly and steadily into a dense bush. Small birds will gather as though by magic, to drink, wash themselves in the spray and preen nearby, or simply to cool off. Choosing dense vegetation is important, to give the little birds some protection from predation at a vulnerable moment.

A pair of Galahs, the female (red iris) preening the male's neck feathers. When any two birds or mated partners preen each other, sometimes simultaneously, it is termed allopreening. This is a very common sight among members of the cockatoo and parrot family. Mungerannie, South Australia

◆ Preening

A bath is usually followed by preening, quick or prolonged. For birds, frequent preening is a constant and essential ritual. Individual feather structure needs to be maintained and groups of feathers re-arranged if some activity has displaced them. Any sticky stuff adhering to the feathers must be carefully removed: blood, fruit sugars, cobwebs—anything that might damage the insulating properties of the plumage or affect the bird in flight. Unwanted particles of dirt or other material, and any ectoparasites (feather lice, mites, louse flies) close to the skin need to be removed. Some good old scratching is also sometimes required.

The bird extracts waxes and oils from the preen glands situated on the coccyx (parson's nose) by rubbing or wiping its beak repeatedly over the glands. It then spreads the compound across its plumage in sweeping movements.

Little wounds may need attention, and bare parts of the legs, toes and soles of the feet need to be cleaned. The vent must be kept spotless. Bills also need to be wiped after eating, especially if the food was meat, fish or carrion, or of a sticky nature—over-ripe fruit, or egg yolk.

Watch for perched birds rubbing their beaks along a branch.

Allopreening

A pleasant occupation indulged in by many pairs of birds of many species is allopreening, used for general pair-bonding as well as for more intense courtship activity. Allopreening is prolonged mutual head and neck nibbling, and also acts as feather care if it reaches areas inaccessible to the preened bird's own beak.

The cockatoos, lorikeets and many other parrots are most often observed at this activity. Entire trees packed with allopreening pairs of Galahs, Little or Long-billed Corellas, or Budgerigars may be seen. Rainbow and Scaly-breasted Lorikeets are also very visible allopreening enthusiasts. The activity reaches a peak during midday siestas in the heat, and before overnight roosting.

Anting, dusting and sunning

These three processes are related to comfort, feather and skin care, and probably anti-ectoparasite measures.

Many passerines engage in 'anting', by either passively allowing ants to enter the plumage, or by actively applying the ants to the feathers, especially under the wings. It is thought that the formic acid given out by the ants is insecticidal.

Many ground-dwelling or ground-frequenting birds dust-bathe. Farmyard chickens, many doves and pigeons and very many Australasian songbirds do it. White-winged Choughs will sometimes be observed in a group, chiselling away in a dry spot under a tree in clay soil. From time to time, individuals pinch up into their beaks the fine powder they have created, and place it under their wings, apparently rubbing it well in, then shaking themselves and creating a cloud of dust. Two things seem to be operating here. Firstly, we think the choughs are exposing the small burrows of ants or termites just beneath the soil surface, and probably eating the occupants. This bit is theoretical, because we have never been close enough to be certain of what we were seeing. The chisellings, the little winding trenches, are there in the soil for all to see. Secondly, when the mood takes them, choughs use the powdery dust to bathe in.

An observation was made recently of Grey Currawongs smearing wet mud on the underparts of their plumage. At first the description sounded like a reversal of dust-bathing. But since some wet muds can smell quite strongly, perhaps the process was similar to 'anting'.

Dust-bathing occurs most often in dry habitats where water is scarce, or where dry soil or clay powder is available on higher points or under tree trunk shelters in forests.

Sunning is deliberate exposure of wing and tail feathers during the hottest part of the day. It is thought to dry the plumage and restore flight-feathers to their original shape. It also helps to control parasites. This is distinct from sun-basking, which involves absorbing heat into the body by choosing a sunny, sheltered location. The bird fluffs the feathers of head and body, exposes its breast to the sunshine with wings held away from the body, or exposes its back with its wings flopped out to the sides. Sometimes a bird may not obviously be sunning or sun-basking, simply spending part of its days in its chosen place in the sun.

It is worth making notes on any of these behaviours you see and, if possible, sketching them or taking photographs.

The need for space

Like humans, some birds need a bit of individual space around them. Watch ducks, coots or moorhens feeding on a pond bank. Watch Bar-tailed Godwits on a sandbar or Silver Gulls on a beach. Every so often one bird will push or run at another bird in

| Spiny-cheeked Honeyeater sunning itself on a warm front porch.

a display of threat, or may actually bite. Individual space varies with species, sex, age and need. Some species tend to be rather solitary during daily and seasonal routines. Others perpetually travel as pairs.

Socially inclined species require less individual space. Birds that huddle together for social and roosting reasons include Laughing Kookaburras, many of the fairy-wrens, members of the miner (manorine) group of honeyeaters, several babbler species, woodswallows (White-breasted, Dusky, and Little Woodswallows in particular), White-winged Chough and Apostlebird. Welcome Swallows sometimes huddle in communal roosts. The White-backed Swallow, Tree Martin and Fairy Martin may enter burrows or nests in numbers.

Record the totals of birds you see in close proximity to each other.

Keeping cool

Birds have a higher body temperature than people. No bird anywhere operates daily at a body (blood) temperature *lower* than a human's, and most routinely are several degrees above. Kiwis, at about thirty-eight degress Centigrade, are generally considered to have the lowest body temperature of any living bird—about the same as a human's normal blood heat. Birds do not perspire, so must find other ways to keep cool in excessively hot weather. They do this by lessening general activity and, during extreme heat, perching quietly in the shade. Many birds reduce their activity in the hotter part of a normal day. Their feathers may be pressed tightly against their bodies to reduce the insulating air space. This is the reverse of fluffing up in cold weather to increase the air trapped beneath feathers. Also, they may bathe, allowing some evaporative cooling to occur, and may drink more frequently.

In hot weather many birds will be seen panting with beaks open or gaping. Some birds achieve accelerated panting by holding the beak open and rapidly vibrating or fluttering the throat and chin region. This 'gular (probably as in 'gullet') fluttering' is easily seen in cormorants, gannets and boobies, frigatebirds and pelicans, because they have bare skin in this region of the body. There is sometimes increased vascularisation in the gular region of these birds. Gular fluttering can sometimes be seen in nestlings and juveniles of bush birds, especially if the small young are partly naked (we saw this in a video about kookaburras). Water vapour and heat are lost by panting and by gular fluttering.

There are a few records of various bush birds in the hot inland entering burrows of rabbits or Hairy-nosed Wombats to escape direct heat in the middle of the day.

Birds frequently shade eggs and nestlings with their body shadow, or with their spread wings.

Seeking cover

Many birds (like humans) prefer to be under cover in extreme weather conditions, which can make birdwatching difficult in windy weather.

During strong winds look for aerial-feeding birds in the lee of tree shelter belts. You may find bee-eaters, cuckoo-shrikes, woodswallows or swallows and martins. Huddling in the lee of banks is a common practice of waterfowl and waders. Ducks, and Hoary-headed and Great Crested Grebes, sometimes cluster in tight rafts on choppy open water, and the rising and falling of the flock, viewed through your binoculars or telescope, can make you feel quite queasy after a while. Gulls often move inland in strong winds and on days of rough seas or heavy rain. They will be found in rain-soaked farm paddocks where earthworms and other creatures have been forced from their little burrows and make easy prey.

Perched birds in strong winds take on a new aerodynamic shape, becoming more 'pointed' as they face into the wind. One evening recently we saw a tall dead tree in an open paddock with a pair of Galahs, a pair of Magpie-larks and a pair of Australian Magpies all perched on separate branches. All were leaning forward, plumage pressed down and really straining just to hold on in the face of a strong sou'west wind.

Increasing wind makes it much harder to both hear and locate small birds in forest environments. And another element can creep in. In 1995, a party of forty BOCA members stayed at Toorour Forest Lodge in the Strathbogie Ranges of central Victoria. We all set out for a late afternoon walk on our first day but rising north winds forced us to beat a very rapid and careful retreat from the forest, as bare sticks and leafy twigs, then large branches and finally several whole trees, began to fall around us. The forest really roars when the big winds come. The birds vanish and it is no place for birdwatchers. Many bush birds lose their nests in strong wind conditions. Some will rebuild or repair them and lay eggs again.

On coastal heaths and grasslands, the small birds hide in deep cover. In the desert and on bare coastal dunes, most birds just leave the scene and seek shelter from wind-driven sand. Occasionally, nesting Pied Oystercatchers, Hooded Plovers or terns will sit tight, allowing the beach sand to bank up against their bodies. Ken recalls seeing Royal, Gentoo and King Penguins in different colonies at Macquarie Island, all with little snow drifts piled around the brooding birds.

White-throated Needletails try to avoid flying into the oncoming wind fronts or storms and, where possible, position themselves in the warm, less turbulent air in advance of the storm. There, the swifts find rising columns of winged ants and termites to feed on. Remaining ahead of the storm, they eventually outpace it, fly around the 'sides' or 'ends' or *perhaps* back over the top, and drop into the more peaceful air behind to resume feeding as opportunity offers.

Going to roost

In the late afternoon offshore, shearwaters gather in a series of large rafts. Then, in the late dusk, they all leave the sea and fly over the coastal breakers to burrows in the sprawling subterranean colony they call home. Little Penguins likewise gather offshore in small groups, then swim ashore and waddle up the beach to nesting burrows on the coastal slopes and dunes. In a few places, human spectators

A large flock of Common Starlings at dusk, swooping in communal flight before roosting.

wait for them. One well-known example is the famous 'Penguin Parade' at Phillip Island in Victoria.

In the Australian inland in their non-breeding season, small groups of White-backed Swallows perform a late-evening flight before diving into burrows for communal roosting.

The introduced Common Starling is well known for the large flocks it forms not long before dark. The birds fly fast, wheeling, breaking up, then reforming the flock again, until all fly to the chosen overnight roost and, with much noise and activity, settle in for the night. Flocks of ravens and Rooks sometimes engage in noisy circling flights just before going to roost.

White-throated Treecreepers often roost overnight inside the lower portions of standing trees which have been partially hollowed out by fire. To sneak up on such trees, having previously discovered that there is a smattering of bird droppings on the floor in a corner of the hollow, to discover that one or two treecreepers are sound asleep in there, snug and warm, holding on vertically to a tiny projection inside the trunk, gives one a delightful sense of achievement, of having attained some bushcraft skills. To sneak away again, leaving the birds undisturbed, is even more worthwhile.

Of course, as darkness falls, night-feeding and night-travelling birds are just setting off on their nocturnal journey.

A Nankeen Kestrel has just alighted on a feeding perch with a skink.
Bundoora, Melbourne

KEN LEADS A DAWN BIRDWATCHING TOUR AT YELLOW WATERS, KAKADU, NORTHERN TERRITORY

Late October. The Dry is still with us. Fogg Dam to the north-west is largely empty, the lowest I have seen it. Plenty of bush birds, but the waterbird numbers were down. Press on to Kakadu. At Cooinda the late afternoon is hot, dusty. The tree and pandanus litter crackles underfoot. But in the heart, the core of the swamp, Yellow Waters is still wet . . .

Embarkation in the pre-dawn gloom. The wide aluminium barge, canopied against the sun to come, putters out into the misted river in a haze of blue fumes. Our guide soon heads off up a long, dark-surfaced backwater. My Japanese birdwatchers are simmering with excitement (or is it resentment?). I made them leave their beloved telescopes in the bus!

The noise from the swamp is exciting, perpetual. Frogs trill and plonk on every possible note of the scale. Fish splash—barramundi, mullet. We are gliding between black banks, bushes and occasional trees in a boat-high fine mist. There is a cacophony of honking calls from hidden Magpie Geese. A hundred or so flying foxes, black, owl-like in flight, pass over silently with deep wing beats. Three tall black shapes stand along the bank, a family of Black-necked Storks. They turn to fly, think better of it, walk out of sight. Black Magpie Geese fly over, ten, twenty, two hundred, maybe a thousand. Everything is black. Black becomes grey, greenish, green. Light comes quickly in the tropics.

Birds are everywhere. We look down the billabong's reach, over a wide, damp, grassy plain full of life and sound. Waterlily patches, a mass of floating flowers. Wide lotus leaves, edges folded and trampled, have little families of red-topped Comb-crested Jacanas trotting about.

We sweat in the humidity with the effort to take it all in. We have time-consuming translation problems in little bursts. Australian White Ibis, Straw-necked Ibis, White-necked Herons, Pied Herons, Glossy Ibis are everywhere. Mud-bespattered Magpie Geese are flying by, lumbering, up-ending and dragging up weed. Great Egrets, Intermediate Egrets, Little Egrets, Cattle Egrets line the banks, walk and wade, spearing little fish in all directions. The Black-necked Storks are fishing too—was that a catfish?

Brolgas, twelve of them, fly across the grassland, pale grey, trailing legs against a green paperbark forest backdrop. Masked Lapwings wheel, stand, run, clatter. A pair of Tawny Frogmouths is suddenly beside us in a dead tree. Small birds surround us, competing for our attention. Forest Kingfishers, a flock of thirty or so Magpie-larks, White-winged and Varied Trillers.

Rainbow Bee-eaters glide over. Two perch in the sun not a boat-length away, jewels on a dead stick. 'Crocodile!' goes a cry and then 'Oh! Did you see *that*?' An egret, perhaps a Little Egret, lingered too long on the edge and 'Whack!', a crocodile's tail crashed into it in a spurt of muddied water, a white flurry, a surge, then widening waves, ripples, quiet. A Little Kingfisher scoots along the dark edge of the bank, a sapphire on wings. Only a few saw it. No second chance.

The sky is throwing birds at us. A pair of White-bellied Sea-Eagles, grey, white, wide-winged, float over, harried by Whistling Kites. Pelicans in a 'V', Pied Herons, a flight of

Wandering Whistling-Ducks with dark heads and straw-coloured wing bars swish by and alight on a pool full of blue lilies, Green Pygmy-geese, Pacific Black Duck and Comb-crested Jacana, all being quartered from the air by fifty or sixty Whiskered Terns.

A dead tree has a Blue-winged Kookaburra, a Forest Kingfisher, four Black Kites. On a broad bare brown bank stand several dozen Australian Pratincoles, long pinkish legs and thin wings folded. A dead log partly in the water is a pedestal for a female Darter, standing in a stretch-winged pose, four Little Black Cormorants and a wide, slimed tortoise. Under branches on the bank are two juvenile Nankeen Night Herons, and a couple of the much smaller Striated Herons, dark blue-grey. Incongruously, there is a Willie Wagtail rattling in the bush.

Every boat length brings more to see: Red-kneed Dotterels, a Caspian Tern, the red-collared variety of Rainbow Lorikeets in a racing little flock, another mass of assorted ibis, Purple Swamphens, Tree Martins on a thin horizontal stick. A stinking dead file snake rolls in our wake. A pair of Pied Butcherbirds, two more Darters, a high-flying Wedge-tailed Eagle, more Green Pygmy-geese in the next pool . . . a group of low-flying Torresian Crows shimmer off towards the distant trees.

My perspiring effort to understand a simple Japanese question is interrupted by two Bar-shouldered Doves, a Sacred Kingfisher, another mass of Magpie Geese, a Brahminy Kite, an even larger crocodile and four more Brolgas . . .

My Japanese party politely clapped the guide as we alighted two hours later, and quickly whisked their telescopes out of the bus. Black-tailed Treecreeper, Rufous-throated Honeyeaters, Lemon-bellied Flycatchers . . .

Yellow Waters, late in the Dry.

White-faced Heron performs a wing-comfort stretch.
Jells Park, Melbourne

CHAPTER EIGHT

Flight

Not all birds fly. The famous Dodo of Mauritius was a huge flightless pigeon, very edible, and a pushover for the European sailors who first encountered it. They caused its extinction within a very few years. Australasia, particularly New Zealand, is well endowed with flightless birds. Loss of flight is believed to be a response to living where birds can gain an adequate food supply without the need for powered flight, and where no predators consistently gain access to them. Some very large birds, the ratites, became flightless. The smallest of their group became flightless and nocturnal. We call them kiwis.

The living flightless birds of Australasia are: introduced Ostrich, plus Emu, Southern Cassowary (Australia and New Guinea), Northern and Dwarf Cassowaries (New Guinea only), Brown Kiwi, Great Spotted Kiwi, Little Spotted Kiwi, Weka, Lord Howe Island Woodhen, Takehe, Kagu (New Caledonia) and Kakapo. Why aren't penguins listed here? Because we strongly contend that penguins *do* fly, with their flippers (that is, wings)—in a thicker medium than air, which we call seawater.

'Ready, steady, go!'

We found a wonderful little phrase in a New Zealand book some time ago: 'Ka maro te kaki o te kawau', or 'Outstretched is the neck of the shag.' The Maoris had noticed that, before a shag (cormorant) took flight it would lean forward and stretch out its neck to signify imminent departure. Maori tradition absorbed this observation and turned it into a formal statement to make at the time when a guest was rising for departure or giving other indications of leaving a social situation.

Birdwatchers will need to be particularly observant with regard to birds taking flight, usually when the observer is spotted by the bird rather than vice versa. You may be doing the right thing, moving cautiously and slowly, but inevitably someone else will suddenly appear around a bend, on the bank of a dam wall, over a dune, or out of the forest into the open, and there will be a whirr of wings as the birds hastily depart.

You must be aware of your surroundings all the time when you are birdwatching. Your performance will be greatly enhanced by taking advantage of any cover in front of you. Keep looking ahead. Anticipate. Be aware that the track turns a corner a hundred metres away. Approach the wall of a low embankment from the best angle to see any birds that may be beyond it. Look slowly from around the wall of a building or over the brow of a sand dune before allowing your whole body to come in sight of any birds there. If you have time, be selective. Look at the most interesting species first, then take in the others.

Once you are attuned to bird behaviour, you will realise that some birds, like the shag, signal their intention to depart. The signal may not always be so obvious, but it is visible nonetheless. Here are some examples:

- Ducks on land begin to walk forward with head held high.
- Cormorants and shags, and the Darter, stretch out their necks as described above.
- Waders and terns will suddenly raise their wings straight up above their backs and stretch, then walk forward, often as a group.
- The Australian Magpie starts to run, raising its wings as it does so.
- Swallows and martins begin to shuffle their feet before flying off a wire or a branch.
- Common Starlings lean forward horizontally on their perch.

If you can interpret the signals given by birds in time, you have the opportunity to back off a bit, stand still, or take another route. Our first duty is not to disturb or give stress to birds unnecessarily. By halting or backing away, you allow the birds to settle and give yourself another chance to observe them quietly.

Begin a notebook entry every time you actually see a bird take flight, and write down just what happens. It will be easier to describe the sequence for large birds than for small birds, which can move very fast. Learning to interpret even some of the signals for some of the species will be very valuable training for you.

Observe and record, in writing or field sketches, the head, wing, tail, leg and any other body movements. Take note of any calls given.

Flapping

Bird flight begins with flapping. The powered stroke of the two wings gives lift and is required to achieve the speed needed for normal flight. The wing in flight presses down on the air beneath it, compressing it and enabling the bird to push hard against the resistance created, thus moving the bird forward. The return stroke in most birds is not powered, so it sideslips through the air with less resistance, ready to push down hard on the air for the next stroke.

The American hummingbirds, distant allies of the swifts, have a powered stroke upwards *and* downwards, so they can hover and manoeuvre very efficiently, and can even fly backwards. Most other birds cannot do this.

Juvenile birds in their early flights sometimes misjudge things, and may be vulnerable to accidents or predators as they try to improve their flying and landing skills.

PARROTS IN FLIGHT

Most people might argue that the colour patterns of parrots are the best way to identify them, but studying their flight mannerisms can also be rewarding.

Long-tailed parrots include the Superb, Princess and Regent Parrots. When you watch the swift flight of parrots such as these, you wonder how anyone can confine that magnificent speed and beauty to a small aviary.

Sulphur-crested Cockatoos are identified by their rounded wings and 'uneven' series of wingbeats (flap, flap, glide certainly, but with strokes of different depths) and they call attention to themselves by their screeching contact calls. Galahs are agile, twisting and turning like paired acrobats in the air.

Gang-gang Cockatoos roll and twist with deep wingbeats as they fly through a stand of trees. But even in open stretches they retain that rocking, rolling flight, like sailors who cannot adjust to walking on dry land.

All the long-tailed, large black-cockatoos have slow, shallow wingbeats, and most wail to each other in flight. Budgerigars can form huge green and yellow flocks and wheel and turn in tight formation. The Red-winged Parrot is a more wary customer with a strong, rocking flight. Recognise them by their plain green heads and their scarlet shoulder patches, which contrast vividly with a deep green back and deep blue rump in the male.

The Swift Parrot breeds in Tasmania and spends winter on the mainland. This is a well-named parrot as its swift, erratic flight is very characteristic (making it hard for beginners to identify). Look for the red underwing coverts in flight, and be sure that it is not a lorikeet.

As a field exercise, when you record the parrot family, include a brief note of their behaviour in the air, especially on occasions when you're not sure of your identification.

Noisy and quiet flight

Noisy-flighted birds—those with stiff-edged wings—can be quite thrilling to hear passing over or near you. A flock of ducks makes a wonderful wing-whistling sound, followed by a swish of feet as they alight on a water surface, and then they all chatter and quack, appearing to express their 'satisfaction' with the manoeuvre. The Australasian Shoveler makes a whirring rather than whistling sound as it flies.

Most pigeons and doves take off from the ground with a whirring clatter of wings, as do most quail and pheasants.

When White-throated Needletails are close by, you can hear a series of rapid slashing 'swishes' in the sky. Tuis have a whirring flight, interspersed with periods of gliding. The male riflebirds in tropical Australia have a somewhat rustling flight, caused by the manner in which they use their rounded wings. An Australian Magpie in a climb to intercept an unwanted intruder, marauder or raptor makes a sharp set of powerful 'swishes' with its wings.

Obviously, soft-flighted birds do not draw themselves to your attention by sound. You are likely to see them coming rather than hear them. The leading edge of the first primary wing feather of, say, a Barn Owl has a fine, comb-like fringe. This breaks up the wind on the powered strokes and there is no sound of swishing. Owls, nightjars, frogmouths and the Owlet-nightjar are in this category.

Flock spacing in flight

An important way of identifying birds that travel in flocks is to learn the appearance of the whole flock for each species, and how individuals move and behave within it. We have to learn 'flock jizz' as well as individual 'bird jizz'. Some birds have different flock behaviours, depending on circumstance, so be prepared to learn several travelling styles for the same species.

For instance, gulls in leisurely flight will travel in loose formation, but if they are moving rapidly towards a target they will close up together in close formation and can mimic a flock of waders. Satin Bowerbirds tend to travel high in a loose or well-spaced flock across gullies and valleys, where their small-headedness, coupled with chesty, dumpy bodies, rounded wings, narrow-waisted tail base and wider, round tail end, can easily be picked out.

In flight, some birds tend to form patterns that are quite consistent in general shape, although not always perfectly maintained. Some form a long string in the sky: Black Swan, the spoonbills, Australasian Gannet, most cormorants and shags, Australian Pelican, Brolga and Sarus Crane. Some fly in 'V' formation: Canada Goose, Australian Shelduck, Australian Pelican, all ibis, Silver and Red-billed Gulls.

Ibis, especially Straw-necked Ibis, often fly in tight flocks, 'vertically-piled stacks' if you like, turning slowly in wheeling circles. We suppose they are soaring, but they are not always in an obvious thermal.

Gliding

Gliding is frequently a component of normal flight once a cruising speed has been achieved. Flap and a longer glide, several flaps and a shorter or longer glide—these are common variations in the flight of birds.

Long gliding flight is a speciality of many seabirds, including albatrosses, most petrels, frigatebirds, pelicans, many raptors, ibis, Brolga, Black-necked Stork, swifts and swiftlets, and the Rainbow Bee-eater. Passerines that frequently glide are woodswallows, swallows and martins. In courtship display, many medium-sized to tiny birds fly up above the territory, then glide down again. Watch for this behaviour and record it.

To be able to stand on a headland, or on the deck of a ship or small boat at sea, and watch albatrosses fly close by is to witness one of the greatest avian sights that the world has to offer. The bird 'points' to the wind with outstretched wings, rising upward virtually to the point of stalling, then falls away in the opposite direction in a raking glide downwind. It then positions itself at right angles to the wind and covers some distance before turning into the wind on a rise once more and repeating the

Three flight pictures: Nankeen Kestrel gliding over tree tops. Bundoora, Melbourne

A Black Kite slowly circles possible prey, constantly and characteristically twisting its tail from side to side. The spread wing tips are sometimes termed 'fingers'. Flinders Ranges, South Australia

A Wedge-tailed Eagle soaring. The great wings and the tail shape are perfectly shown. Despite backlighting, the amount of golden plumage suggests a younger bird. Adults become blacker with age.

process all over again. The wings rarely flap. The close-up visible motion consists mostly of countless tiny adjustments of the outstretched wings.

Birdwatchers rely on the constant course changes of albatrosses and most smaller petrel species to give them sufficient views of the dorsal and ventral patterns (especially the underwing pattern) to make an identification. Many species can be reliably identified at extreme range. Others can only be reliably recognised by very close inspection indeed.

Soaring

Many species that glide in the course of normal flight are also capable of greatly extending their glide in the form of soaring. Here, rising air currents are exploited to give buoyancy, and progress is made across country in a series of upward spirals, fast or slow, and often to a great height. Once it has arrived at the top of a thermal column, in a long, straight or gently downward glide, or with some powered flight, the bird transfers to the next column of rising air. In this way much distance is covered with minimal effort. Remember that soaring is an outcome of rising air over heated land, and therefore doesn't take place very early in the morning.

Look for soaring birds in the heat of a calm day. Some examples are frigatebirds, Australian Pelican, White-necked Heron, all ibis, the 'inland' cormorants, especially the Little Pied Cormorant; also the Darter, Brolga, Sarus Crane, Black-necked Stork, many raptors (especially the large kites and the eagles), Silver Gull, White-throated Needletail and Fork-tailed Swift.

Record, over an entire year, the time of day at which you saw birds soaring. Which species were they?

Hovering

Hovering is a specialised form of flight in which the body sinks to a tail-down, almost vertical position. The tail is fully spread and the wings beat at such a rate as to compensate precisely for airflow and achieve sufficient lift to remain exactly in one place.

Examples amongst birds of prey are Black-shouldered and Letter-winged Kite, Brown Falcon, Nankeen Kestrel and Barn Owl. Ken has seen Barn Owls by moonlight hovering over wheat paddocks in north-west Victoria. Small passerines that briefly hover include several thornbill and gerygone species (including Grey Warbler in New Zealand) and Weebill, Eastern and Western Spinebill, some other honeyeaters, and the Olive-backed Sunbird.

'Diving' in or through the air

'Diving' is not a good word to use here. Diving into water is not the same as diving in a steep aerial glide. With falcons we use a special word: we speak of the 'stoop' of a Peregrine, Black or Grey Falcon, New Zealand Falcon, Australian Hobby and

A hovering Black-shouldered Kite, viewed from below. The wide-spread and drooped tail, wide-open primary feathers and projecting false wing, or, alula on each side, indicate an almost complete 'stop' in the air. The bird's eyes are turned downward, the entire body 'pivotting' around the eyes until a drop on to the prey is commenced. The retracted talons are closed tightly. When the legs are extended to strike, the talons open, then close shut as the weight of the kite's body comes down and folds up the legs once more. The prey is crushed. Port Campbell National Park, Victoria

Nankeen Kestrel. This usually means a hunting pass at great speed down on to prey. Little Eagle, Wedge-tailed Eagle and some other raptors perform a repetitive diving and rising display flight in the air as part of courtship behaviour. So does the White-throated Needletail. The migratory Dollarbird throws itself around the sky when hawking for insects, even more so for territorial and courtship purposes. It is one of a group of eleven species spread through Africa and across Asia that have earned themselves the collective name of 'rollers'.

'Whiffling'

A number of strong-flying birds have the ability to descend rapidly out of the sky. They include several ducks (but especially Australian Wood Duck and Australian Shelduck), the Little Black and Little Pied Cormorants, many species of waders and some gulls, Sulphur-crested Cockatoo, Long-billed and Little Corellas, and Galah. A flying flock will sometimes conclude a flight by suddenly 'putting on the brakes' in the air. Birds go in all directions, often calling excitedly, diving down with erratic side-slipping flight, occasionally rolling right over onto their backs, and all literally plummeting down out of the sky to pull up and land lightly together at the desired spot or on a water surface. The roar of wings can be very loud. We believe that the word used in Britain for this activity is 'whiffling'.

Diving into water

A number of seabirds dive headlong into water to seize prey. The gannets and boobies are best known for this.

Of interest is the fact that when gannets dive down and miss taking prey on the first strike, they can kick out with their feet and chase fish. They also half fold their wings and use them as well to increase speed and sort of 'fly' after the fish, all of which gives them a second chance to catch something. Gannets behaving in this way were first seen (and photographed) by divers working under oil rig platforms in Bass Strait in 1974. Shearwaters use their wings to fly under water in the same way—it is easy to see the similarity to penguins' flippers.

Shearwaters sit on the water surface, often in large flocks, and repeatedly duck-dive, 'flying' down through the water with their wings before re-emerging at the surface.

On Bass Strait's shores a few years ago, Ken sat with some other birdwatchers on a sand dune watching just beyond the surf line where plunging Australasian Gannets were immediately followed into the water by Fluttering Shearwaters. As each gannet vanished, several shearwaters would rush to the spot, alight momentarily, then also duck-dive and vanish. The shearwaters were probably seeking smaller prey, perhaps mysid shrimps or the like, which had been flushed into activity or greater visibility by the gannets. This action would appear to be akin to the commensal behaviour shown by Cattle Egrets, Willie Wagtails and Common Starlings towards stock in a paddock.

Propulsion under water is either by the use of wings, as described in the examples, or by the feet, which are used for underwater propulsion by grebes, diving and dabbling ducks, coots and some other species such as cormorants, shags and the Darter.

Azure and Little Kingfishers use their wings under water, too, as they briefly pursue tiny fish and other aquatic organisms.

Picking prey off the water surface

Many species that fly above the sea, or over water surfaces such as lakes or sewage ponds, dip down to pick up food items, but remain airborne as they do it. First candidates here are the storm-petrels, the frigatebirds and tropicbirds, skuas and jaegers, some gulls and most terns; also swallows and martins.

Another bunch of surface 'clutchers' are the fishing raptors: Osprey, Black, Whistling and Brahminy Kites, and White-bellied Sea-Eagle (which, incidentally, is really a kite too).

Feeding from the surface

Examples of birds that alight on the water surface then reach for food are Magpie Goose, Mute Swan, Black Swan, some diving ducks, also Blue Duck (New Zealand),

A Swamp Harrier coursing low to hunt over lake reed beds and other herbage, then gliding to a landing. Its wide wings enable slow, low soaring and lifting of heavy prey. Around it are Black-winged Stilts and many Black Swans. In New Zealand, the common Australasian Harrier (Kahu) behaves in the same way. Despite its name, it is exactly the same species as the Australian bird and is widespread across islands of the western Pacific region. Bool Lagoon, South Australia

dabbling ducks such as Pacific Black (Grey) Duck, Mallard and teal; Australian Pelican, albatrosses, giant-petrels.

Sieve-feeding (or filter-feeding) birds include the shovelers and the Pink-eared Duck; also the oceanic prions.

Those that consistently dive for food are the several diving ducks (Blue-billed, Musk, Hardhead and New Zealand Scaup), penguins, shearwaters, diving-petrels and some other petrels, all grebes, gannets (again), cormorants and shags, Darter, and Eurasian Coot.

A pair of Southern Whitefaces perched over a broken tree branch which may contain a small hollow suitable for breeding in. Note the combination of facial markings, which always make these tiny acanthizids look as though they are 'unhappy'. Rainbow Valley, Northern Territory

CHAPTER NINE

Breeding behaviour

There are a great many bird species in which adult males and females are of similar colouring, making the sexes practically indistinguishable in the field (unless they have different calls or you actually see them mating). A few random examples might be Sooty Shearwater, White-faced Storm-Petrel, Baillon's Crake, Red-necked Stint, Northern Rosella, Shining Bronze-cuckoo, Western Thornbill, Rufous-banded Honeyeater, Apostlebird, Dunnock, Singing Bushlark and Silvereye.

But why do male and female birds of some species have different plumage patterns? Not just to make life more interesting for birdwatchers, that's for sure. Female birds are usually attracted to the brightest males.

Sight is the dominant sense in birds. They cannot fly without it and it is also their primary tool when searching for food, or when trying to identify mates, family members, or predators. Most birds have a very complex appreciation of colour, especially with regard to the subtleties of blue-green and yellow-green (this may help them to discriminate by sight between different vegetation types). Birds have better colour vision than mammals, including humans.

Males and females of the same species are sometimes different in appearance and size. This is 'sexual dimorphism' which, quite apart from basic internal anatomy, refers to differences between plumage colour, or to a variety of other physical features.

Blatant sexual dimorphism

Examples of species that have obvious plumage differences between male and female are Peafowl, California Quail, Paradise Shelduck, Australian Wood Duck, Mallard, phalaropes (*breeding* plumage only), Superb Lyrebird, many of the Australian malurids (fairy-wrens and their allies), Scarlet, Red-headed and Black Honeyeaters, Western Spinebill, Shining Flycatcher, White-winged Triller, Regent and Satin Bowerbirds, Figbird, Tomtit, Stitchbird, Olive-backed Sunbird and Common Blackbird.

The Eclectus Parrot has a stunning reversal of the normal 'bright male–dull female' trend in parrots, in that the female is bright red and blue, the male green.

Less obvious sexual dimorphism

There are many other species in which plumage dimorphism is present but not so obvious, as when the females are softer in colouring than the males. Where the female does most of the brooding, plumage that blends with the dominant colours of her habitat will obviously be of advantage. Parrots, which nest in hollows, are a family that has less need of this kind of camouflage.

A few examples showing other minor plumage variations are the Wandering Albatross (old adult females at Macquarie Island have a grey smudge on the crown, while males' crowns are pure white), Red-capped Plover, Shore Plover, Nankeen Kestrel (the female has a rufous rump), Eastern Rosella, Laughing Kookaburra (older males often have a blue rump), all the Australian treecreepers (chest and face markings differ), Striated Grasswren, Gilbert's Whistler, Australian Magpie, Cirl Bunting and Redpoll.

A number of species are sexually dimorphic with regard to features other than plumage. Examples of dimorphism in bill length are Royal Penguin (males have larger bills), Bar-tailed Godwit (males have shorter bills) and of course the extinct Huia would have been an example, too (females had much longer bills). Male and female Bar-tailed Godwits differ in leg length.

Some species show dimorphism in the colours of their 'soft parts': Emu (bare skin of neck), Australian Pelican and Great Frigatebird (rich red skin of throats of breeding males), Eurasian Coot (head shield differences), differing facial skin colour of Figbird sexes, Common Starling (bluish bill base in breeding males, pink in breeding females).

Regent Bowerbirds. This group of birds has two fully mature males, a changeling male with a yellow bill and eye, and three slightly larger dark-billed females at left. O'Reilly's, Lamington National Park, Queensland

Satin Bowerbirds: an excellent example of dichromatic plumage (sexual dimorphism). The plumage of the adult male Satin Bowerbird is an even deep metallic blue colour, appearing black in dull light. The billiant blue eye and pale bill indicate maturity. Fraser National Park, Victoria

The dorsal plumage of the adult female of the Satin Bowerbird is olive green. The chin and throat are pale creamy-brown and the flanks are strongly scalloped. The wings are brown but in flight a rich tan colour shows in the underwing. The brilliant blue eye and dark bill indicate maturity. Fraser National Park, Victoria

Black Swan, Weka and Brown Songlark are three amongst the very many species that are sexually dimorphic with regard to general body size, the males being larger than the females. This is, of course, a very common feature in many animals. The male Black Swan in a mated pair always carries his head higher than does the female. Go to a pond and have a look.

Not so common is the sexual difference in which females are larger than males. A few examples (there are others) could be the kiwis, some of the kites, Red Goshawk, the harriers and most falcons, some owls (Southern Boobook; Morepork and Little Owl in New Zealand; Lesser Sooty and Sooty Owls; Barn, Grass and Masked Owls), also Pheasant Coucal and White-throated Nightjar.

These are only a few varieties and examples of sexual dimorphism; you will find many more examples in your field guide.

Courtship

The breeding cycle begins with courtship. During the courtship phase of the breeding cycle you may see:
- larger numbers of individual birds of all species in any area
- a much higher level of general bird sound in the air, punctuated by a variety of recognisable territorial songs or challenges

- many intense local squabbles breaking out
- energetic flying chases through the trees, across a water surface or around the margins of ponds and farmland
- aerial diving displays of raptors, swifts, drongos, larks, cisticolas
- an increased amount of allopreening, particularly by the parrot family.

From the beginning of the breeding season, watch for examples of courtship displays. Look for male Musk Ducks in a splashing 'steaming display'. If you are lucky enough to be near a sub-Antarctic island, you may see the beautiful synchronised or parallel flying display of the Light-mantled Sooty Albatross. The famous 'water dance' of a pair of courting Great Crested Grebes is very spectacular. Dusky Moorhens and Eurasian Coots chase members of their own species aggressively on the water surface, showing several interesting postures as they do so. Tasmanian Native-hens, and Pukekos (Purple Swamphens) engage in aggressive running and chasing displays on the banks of lakes, and in crops and pasture. All these behaviours are partly courtship and partly territory dispute.

Look for the rising and falling aerial displays of some raptors, and also the 'food pass' display, in which the male passes food or drops it to a female flying below. Out in the grasslands and wide shallow swamps, Brolga 'dance' in high-stepping display. In open arid country, the male Australian Bustard has a wonderful display with an extended throat sac, which is swung and swayed as the bird emits deep drawn-out boomings.

On sanctuary islands in New Zealand's far south, male Kakapo, the rare nocturnal parrots, gather nightly to 'boom' to each other for weeks at a time as part of the mating preparations. Such groupings are called 'lek' displays. Male lyrebirds increase their vocal and 'dancing' displays on their mounds. Since they are essentially winter breeders, this begins in autumn. Spangled Drongo males have a high-flying aerial display, involving a deep dive with wings held up and tail cocked. To attract females, male riflebirds perform wing-snapping dances on top of bare poles in the forest.

Male bowerbirds accelerate the degree of display in and about their bower or court. The amazing collections of objects they bring to a court is well worth examination, but please do not take anything or interfere with its arrangement. The bird has already put everything *exactly* where he wants it.

Grey Butcherbirds become very vocal in the southern Australian states in the autumn and winter months before breeding. Skylarks produce a series of long-sustained aerial flights to great heights above the nest site, singing as they rise.

Nests, mounds, bowers, courts and roosts

Courtship displays are often connected with nest building. Presentation of nesting materials is one such ploy. Behaviour that is part of preparing a nest may also become a display to attract or retain the interest of a mate. Male Australasian Gannets

The courtship bower of a Great Bowerbird. The central aisle is fairly clear of items, but piled around are bleached land snail shells and coral fragments. The male displays to, and if possible mates with, any females who come to the bower in the breeding season. The females then go off to build a conventional stick nest somewhere, raising the young alone. Groote Eylandt, Gulf of Carpentaria, Northern Territory

cart in seaweed and offer it graciously. Australian finches perform 'stem displays' with long wisps of grass.

Stick-carrying is an obvious sign of nest-building activity and some species, such as pigeons, ibis and herons, are more easily observed than others. Magpies, crows, ravens and currawongs begin their nest-building activities from mid-winter onward. White-winged Chough families set about the early construction of mud nests, then let them dry for several weeks. Sometimes old nests from previous years are refurbished as well. Galahs line their nests with freshly picked sprays of leaves, and one sign of courtship is a Galah waving a leafy twig around in the air.

Young birds in their first breeding season are often unsuccessful because they have not perfected the techniques of courtship and nest building. They may build nests in unsuitable locations and abandon them at any stage of the cycle.

Several bird species build structures that are not nests at all. Male lyrebirds prepare display mounds, approximately one metre wide discs of bare earth, scattered throughout their territory. Some bowerbirds build elaborate vertical structures of sticks and other vegetation, with a central passage through which the male bird dances, displaying to and mating with as many females as he can attract. This is the bower. The Tooth-billed Bowerbird ('The Stagemaker') clears a 'court' on the forest floor.

Throughout their territories, members of the babbler family build large, untidy stick nests with side entrances, using them to roost at night in a communal huddle, and eventually breeding in one of them.

Copulation

The ultimate act of copulation follows a varying amount of increasingly intensive preparation (seduction?) of the female by the male. Once a decision to mate has been reached, the copulating act itself is usually quick. The male in practically every species eventually flies or clambers onto the female's back, their two cloacal openings are pressed together for a mere second or two and ejaculation of sperm takes place. The act can be performed silently, or with a considerable amount of noise and ker-fuffle. The purpose of copulation is to enable the male to fertilise the female ovum.

In polygamous species (such as lyrebirds, bowerbirds and riflebirds), a single male competes for the attention of as many females as he can. Having allowed copulation to take place, the females take full responsibility for nesting, brooding and rearing the offspring.

Young males may need several seasons to practice their seduction techniques. In winter you might see immature male lyrebirds practising their display. Young male riflebirds take a season or so to perfect their wing-snapping seduction. Male Satin Bowerbirds do not mature into adult male plumage until about seven years old, so they have plenty of time to practise bower making.

Sometimes the weather interferes. At Macquarie Island, in late September and early October, Ken would see male Royal Penguins hopefully clambering aboard their prone females, only to be repeatedly blown straight off again by the roaring winds which so frequently blow there. Each time, the males landed upside down on the rocks or wet sand but, undaunted, would laboriously attempt the operation over and over again.

Nest building

Nests are diverse in form, construction, placement and durability, ranging from a shallow scrape in the sand to the complicated woven nest of a Mistletoebird. But mention 'bird's nest', and most people immediately think of a nice little round cup-shaped nest, attractively finished and tucked superbly into a suitable bush or hanging tree foliage: the nest of a songbird.

Many hazards stand between bird parents and a successfully fledged brood. Delicate nests, built at the end of thin branches for safety from predators, may be the

Pied Oystercatchers engaged in copulation on an open beach. Note the red bilaterally compressed bill, typical of oystercatchers. Griffith Island, Port Fairy, western Victoria

Single egg of a Pied Oystercatcher on a sand bank. Lake Victoria, eastern Victoria

An adult Fairy Martin busy adding to the entrance spout (neck) of its bottle-shaped mud nest. This group of nests is under the overhang of an old leaning tree. The structure shows off the hundreds of globules of saliva-soaked mud necessary to build each structure. The bright rufous crown of the Fairy Martin is diagnostic (the closely related Tree Martin has a black crown). Mildura, Victoria

first to blow down in strong winds. Sittellas build a deep nest to prevent the eggs being rolled out in a gale. Flooding of the bottom of the nest must be avoided. Nests in tree-hollows as well as nests in wetlands may suffer from unseasonal heavy rain.

Concealment is vital, to protect parents and young during incubation and brooding. Concealment may be effected by placing nest material inside a hole in a bank or a tree, or by various methods of camouflage. A careful construction in the fork of a small branch, for example, can blend so well with the bark that the nest is almost invisible. However, this may not deter predators that hunt by scent, taste or thermal receptors, such as some mammals and snakes.

Birds that rely on stillness and camouflage to protect them when brooding may be extremely vulnerable to predation from introduced animals against which they have almost no defences.

When birds nest in colonies, the nests are referred to as 'colonial' nests. Here, there is no attempt at concealment. Sheer weight of numbers is their protection.

Some nest types and some birds that build them

As a guide for beginners we have compiled a list of the typical nest sites and structures, and the birds that nest in these ways.

Mounds

Brush-turkeys, Malleefowl and Scrubfowl are the 'megapodes' or 'mound-builders', famous as constructers of large piles of vegetation and soils, in which eggs are incubated by heat of fermentation.

The adult male of the Australian Brush-turkey and Malleefowl, and both male and female of the Orange-footed Scrubfowl, regulate the heat from outside the mound by manipulating the pile of litter and the overburden above it.

Burrows

Little Penguin, many shearwaters, petrels, diving-petrels, storm-petrels. Kiwis, Kea and Little Owl (*often* use burrows), some kingfishers, Rainbow Bee-eater, Spotted, Red-browed, Striated and (some) Forty-spotted Pardalotes, White-backed Swallow.

Surface nests—colonial or sub-colonial species

Most larger penguins, giant-petrels, some albatrosses, gannets and boobies, pelicans, frigatebirds, many long-legged water birds (ibis and heron families), cormorants and shags, Darter, some waders (Banded Stilt), gulls and terns.

Surface nests—solitary species

Emu, Southern Cassowary, Pied Stilts, oystercatchers, stone-curlews, many plovers and dotterels, lapwings, pratincoles, Caspian Tern.

On cliffs and ledges

Falcons (if the sites are suitable).

Under cliffs and ledges

Welcome Swallow, martins.

Inside hollow trees or branches

Most cockatoos and parrots, most owls, Owlet-nightjar, Dollarbird, some pardalotes, Yellowhead, Tree Martin (occasionally Fairy Martin, Welcome Swallow), Laughing Kookaburra, House Sparrow, Gouldian Finch, Common Starling and Common Myna.

Holes drilled in arboreal termitaria

Several kingfishers, Blue-winged Kookaburra.

Tunnels in terrestrial termitaria
Some small parrots—Hooded, Golden-shouldered and (formerly) Paradise Parrots. Buff-breasted Paradise-Kingfisher; Gouldian Finch (at times).

Branch surface, no nest
White Tern.

Stick nests in trees—colonial birds
Cormorants and shags, Darter. Also many long-legged water birds (the heron and ibis families).

Stick nests in trees—large solitary-breeding birds
Great-billed Heron, Black-necked Stork, Osprey, eagles and kites.

Completely dark caves
Grey-rumped Swiftlet.

Cave entrances
(twilight zone; this category may include some mines, culverts, drains)
Masked Owl, Rockwarbler (Origma), Grey Shrike-thrush (occasionally), Welcome Swallow, Tree and Fairy Martins, Common Starling and Common Myna.

Floating nests
Grebes are the obvious ones. Dusky Moorhens, Eurasian Coots, jacanas, Whiskered Terns and others may sometimes find themselves entering this category, thanks to rising waters in a swamp somewhere.

Freely suspended nests
Yellow-throated Scrubwren, Brown Gerygone, some other gerygones including Grey and Chatham Island Warblers, Brown-backed Honeyeater, Olive-backed Sunbird, Mistletoebird.

Small suspended cradles
Many small honeyeaters.

Large suspended cradles
Spangled Drongo, Yellow and Olive-backed Orioles, Figbird.

Untidy open stick nests in trees or shrubs
Many doves and pigeons, Australia's wattlebirds, and friarbirds, whistlers and shrike-thrushes, woodswallows, butcherbirds, Australian Magpie, currawongs, Kokako, ravens, crows and Rook, catbirds and bowerbirds.

White-naped Honeyeater at a typically situated nest, a hanging cradle in outer foliage of a eucalypt.

Brown-backed Honeyeater's suspended nest in a paperbark (Melaleuca). This nest has recently been abandoned. This honeyeater is almost the exclusive host of the Brush Cuckoo in north eastern Queensland. Town Common, Townsville, Queensland

The small White-plumed Honeyeater (Greenie) on its suspended cup nest. In inland Australia, it is especially found in association with large Red Gums and other eucalypts growing on the banks of watercourses (riparian vegetation). West of the Warrumbungle Ranges, north central New South Wales

A male Emu with a large collection of eggs.
Note the fascinating way the bird sits (crouches).

Untidy dome-shaped stick nests with side entrances
Babblers, and (being generous) Metallic Starling.

Small cup-shaped nests in trees or shrubs
Silvereyes .

Large neat cup-shaped nests in trees or shrubs
Common Blackbird, Song Thrush.

With interesting nest decorations
Australo-Papuan robins (lichen), Crested Bellbird (processional caterpillars), riflebirds (sloughed-off snake skin).

Brood platforms
Following successful breeding in a conventional nest, Tasmanian Native-hens build roosting platforms to which they move their recently hatched chicks. These are considered to be brooding platforms, rather than nests. The true nest, used to lay, incubate and hatch the eggs, is usually abandoned. Purple Swamphens (Pukeko) also use roosting platforms.

Egg-laying and incubation

Once an egg is fertilised, there is a pause of several hours, or a day or two in the bigger birds, while the shell gland at the lower end of the oviduct lays down the hard, crystalline calcareous eggshell, decorated with distinctive colours for each species and given a granulated, glossy or chalky surface.

The total number of eggs normally laid by a female is known as 'the clutch'.

Egg shapes vary from pointed at one end (pyriform: some gulls) through several variations of the oval (most birds) to almost rounded (spherical: some parrots, owls, kingfishers and others).

Incubation (brooding) is a waiting game, with many variations in duration, parental attendance, and the need to protect eggs from heat, cold, desiccation, or potential predators.

A few species of birds lay eggs that are disproportionately larger or smaller than their body size.

Nestlings that hatch with a full, dense covering of down take longer in incubation, therefore the egg has to contain more nutrients to tide the embryo over for a longer time. A few examples (there are others) are Emu, Southern Cassowary, kiwis, quail and pheasants, megapode chicks, all waterfowl, grebes, albatrosses and petrels, most waders, skuas, gulls and terns. On the other hand, most birds hatch a naked, helpless little creature. In pelicans, cormorants and shags, the entire cockatoo and parrot group, cuckoos, kingfishers, and almost all passerines or songbirds, the egg is incubated for a shorter period and the parents have to feed nestlings intensively to provide energy for growth.

Can bird species be recognised by their eggs, or from scraps of eggshell?

Yes, many can! For example, Emu eggshell can be found lying in the desert of Australia in all sorts of places, and is a common component of recent fossil sites. Certain birds have highly distinctive or coloured eggs and scraps of these are readily identifiable. But please do not allow the notion that you can begin to identify eggs in nests lead you into the path of egg collection. *Do not collect eggs*. It is not fair, it is not necessary, it is not legal. The birds need their eggs more than you do.

Imprinting and hatching

Imprinting is necessary so that juveniles can recognise their own parent or parents and reject or avoid others. Imprinting can begin before the egg is hatched, or during hatching, when whistlings from the chick are replied to by the parent birds. After hatching, the behaviour and plumage of attendant adults are imprinted on the young bird and this ensures that it will seek mates of its own kind.

Imprinting is a learned behaviour, which is why some hand-reared nestlings have imprinted on humans. In the first months of life the juvenile bird is highly sensitive to minute differences in sound as well as appearance and is able to learn the 'correct' songs and calls of its parents.

Independent hatchlings

Young megapodes do not obviously imprint on any other bird. They emerge from the buried egg, and dig their way to the surface and out of the mound. They know 'Yes, I am a megapode', and 'This is what megapodes do' and they scoot off into the surrounding vegetation to fend for themselves.

Dependent nestlings

We could write kilometres of text on this subject but will simply say that the *majority* of the world's birds need some parental care from the moment of hatching onward. A pair of birds sharing the responsibilities of rearing young is considered the normal pattern. Co-operative breeding is an important aspect of breeding in *some* species.

The real exceptions fall into a wide range of categories, but it is really to do with technique, sequence and method, rather than radical differences in treatment of nestlings. Cuckoos, described below, are certainly exceptions. So are the many species in which males are polygamous, mating with several or more females. The females, once mated, go off to build nests and rear the young alone (Superb Lyrebird, probably Albert's Lyrebird, the various bowerbirds (but not the catbirds), riflebirds and certainly many of New Guinea's birds of paradise).

Male Emu and Cassowary are responsible for raising the young alone, as are Painted Snipe. (Male Emperor Penguins are left alone with the eggs throughout the Antarctic winter, but the females return in time to feed the hatchlings and so are included in the normal group above.)

Helpers at the nest

Co-operative 'communal' breeding, or 'helpers at the nest', provides improved food delivery when several birds in a 'family party' help to raise the young. Some eighty Australian bird species are communal breeders, although the degree of co-operation does vary.

To prove co-operative breeding, you must look for *three* birds or more, all in sight at once, and all clearly supplying food to nestlings or fledglings. You have to be sure that birds in addition to the two parents are involved.

The best-known co-operative breeders are Laughing and Blue-winged Kookaburras, all treecreepers other than White-throated, virtually all of the beautiful little fairy-wrens, emu-wrens and grasswrens; possibly the Weebill, certainly the Bell Miner and other manorine honeyeaters, some of the White-naped Honeyeater 'group', babblers, Varied Sittella, Figbird, Australian Magpie, White-winged Chough and Apostlebird.

Do not confuse co-operative breeding with *colonial* breeding, where close-packed or loosely grouped birds, above or below ground, are raising only their own chicks.

CUCKOOS

Cuckoos are birds worthy of considerable study. They don't attract a very good press, being parasitic by nature. Probably more is surmised about them than is really known. To study cuckoo behaviour in the field and to report it accurately would be a very worthy aim for new birdwatchers. Cuckoos will keep you busy for years.

Their calls are diagnostic and you will probably hear them before you see them. Cuckoos arrive as adults in a region, possibly the same birds in the same general breeding area each year (do they, like salmon, return to their birthplace to breed?). There is little, if any, proof that this happens, as too few cuckoos have been banded and then recovered.

Cuckoos lay eggs that are astonishingly small in relation to the bulk of the female. Females appear to watch nesting birds and usually enter the host's nest to lay the second or third egg of a clutch, removing one of the host's eggs at the same time to keep the number correct. The colour of the cuckoo's egg closely matches the eggs of the host. It is just possible (not confirmed) that two eggs with the shell on are produced daily by the cuckoo.

The naked young cuckoo, on hatching, soon manages to heave out all other eggs or nestlings. It feeds avidly and induces not only the foster parents but also other birds to bring food. The list of the host species for each cuckoo is very long.

Cuckoos can be neatly divided into three groups in Australasia. We have medium-sized parasitic cuckoos of the Oriental, Brush, Pallid and Fan-tailed group. The small-sized bronze-cuckoo group has representatives from Africa to the Pacific. Much larger species are the Koel, the Long-tailed and the Channel-billed Cuckoo.

When identifying cuckoos on the *tip* of Cape York Peninsula, in Far North Queensland, you have to be aware that the large male Koel, all black and shiny, in general appearance greatly resembles the smaller Spangled Drongo and Trumpet Manucode, also all black and shiny. But it is only an issue in this relatively small region where the ranges of the three species overlap.

We are not sure to what extent nestling cuckoos imprint on any of the eager hosts or other species valiantly bringing food. We wonder (unknowing but game to speculate) whether the parent cuckoos meet up with their offspring in the district in which they were hatched. We ask because once (at Wingan Inlet, eastern Victoria) we saw two fully adult Horsfield's Bronze-Cuckoos feeding an obvious juvenile of the same species. We ask also because in south-eastern Queensland two years ago, for several days running, we saw two large juvenile Channel-billed Cuckoos, squawking loudly, accompanying two adult birds in regular flights across a valley.

Nest sanitation

Some species keep their nests very clean by removing eggshell fragments soon after hatching and dumping them at a safe distance from the nest. Droppings of the nestlings are also removed regularly.

In other species this never happens. Nestlings are expected to void over the edge of the nest. The noticeable smell around the nests of fish-eating birds such as gannets and cormorants is partly created by the accumulation of fishy droppings (guano).

Crèches

A number of species organise their fledglings into groups of young birds, sometimes supervised by a few older birds, while the various parents go off and forage for food. Crèches are used by some penguins. Galahs also have a crèche system for their newly fledged young.

First flight

'Fledging' is defined as 'taking the first flight' or 'leaving the nest for the first time'. This is a very dangerous period in a young bird's life. The first flight and those following are frequently precarious affairs. Wing muscles, despite flapping practice on the edge of the nest, are not fully tested. Full flying speed may not be achieved quickly. Most flying birds are 'L'-platers for a few days, then, if all goes well, will be safely up and away soon after. There are plenty of exceptions. And there are other hazards beyond the mechanical.

Ken once stood with a fellow birdwatcher in front of the broad cliff overhang of the Upper Erskine River, known far and wide as Swallow Cave, in the Otway Ranges of Victoria. The two watched as, every few minutes, another fledgling Tree Martin (the 'swallows' of Swallow Cave) would teeter to the edge of its muddy nest, leap into space, fly shakily perhaps ten, fifteen or twenty metres, then be snapped up whole by one or other of a pair of Laughing Kookaburras, which, perfectly positioned in nearby trees and obviously well-practised, took every single one.

Play in young birds

There can be no doubt that some young birds indulge in forms of play. It is more obvious in those species where co-operative breeding exists. Large downy juvenile penguins of several species in crèches in the sub-Antarctic and Antarctic sometimes chase each other about, bumping and cannoning off others—apparently doing it for pleasure, not hostility. Galahs have occasionally been recorded repeatedly sliding down playground slides in a park or in kindergarten grounds. They have also been seen sliding down obliquely placed stanchions or supporting cables, treating them like 'banisters'.

At different times and in widely spaced localities, Ken has seen juvenile White-winged Chough, Apostlebird, Australian Magpie and Grey Currawong youngsters rolling on the ground and kicking each other, sometimes locking claws and lying on their sides for several seconds at a time, before resuming the 'play'.

Southern Scrub-robin. A nestling, still very dependent on its parents, but on the way to fledging. The thin whitish centres to the body feathers give the bird the typical 'baby robin' striations on this, its first (juvenile) plumage. Kingower, north-west Victoria

A well-grown but clearly juvenile Chough was once seen repeatedly tapping a broken scrap of bottle glass on a steel fence post, apparently enjoying the tinkling sound it made. A family party of Choughs will sometimes swing on pendent objects, jumping on and off, and seem to be doing it for pleasure. Once in a while such behaviour leads to toes being entangled and a lingering death. If White-winged Choughs come to your garden, make sure they cannot come to harm when swinging. Other examples of play are known, and some have been published.

We think that birdwatchers who observe such activities as these should interpret them if possible, and record them. It is generally considered a sin to be too anthropomorphic in such descriptions, so please temper your records with good science.

What happens to old nests?

Songbirds' nests are usually abandoned after use. Some may be used for second broods, or they may gradually fall apart. If situated in an ideal location this can take years. Many nests are recycled or raided for spare parts. Lining materials are often used more than once. Some become home to different species entirely, not always birds. Most old nests eventually fall apart, are blown down, or are washed away.

Nest etiquette for birdwatchers

Strictly limit your visits to any nest sites. Eggs may readily be deserted; hatchlings too. There is a very real danger of attracting predators to a nest by leaving human scent on or about the nest site.

Male Mistletoebird at its suspended 'purse-shaped' nest in an exotic garden, the fine silky composition being largely spider web. The brown beads are caterpillar droppings.

Do not linger near nests. Do not leave litter, obvious tracks or other clues for predators (or predatory people) to find. Feral animals such as foxes, and possibly wild pigs, understand human behaviour and will investigate traces of human scent. Brush-tailed Possums in Australia and various introduced mammals in New Zealand sometimes take eggs and young birds from nests.

When you find nests in the open, move away slowly and deliberately. Do not panic adult surface ground-nesters (penguins, gannets and boobies, cormorants or shags, pelicans, ibis, gulls, terns), as predators (frigatebirds, Pukeko, hawks, skuas, gulls, ravens) can then attack eggs and young. Similarly, do not keep ground-nesting species away from their nests by staying nearby. Thermal stress builds rapidly in eggs and small chicks. Never allow your dog near ground-nesting birds.

Do not blunder through burrowed areas where seabirds such as penguins, the various shearwaters (Short-tailed, Sooty, Flesh-footed or Wedge-tailed) or White-faced Storm-Petrels have nests. Observe sanctuary signs, keep to marked tracks or approach only to the very edge of the colony. If you cause a collapse, eggs, nestlings or adults can all be smothered, and predators or rain can enter. If possible, you must *immediately* dig out and repair a burrow roof you have collapsed. Use driftwood, or some other material. Make it safe.

Do not linger close by at night, when nocturnal parents are returning to burrows. Watch and listen to the proceedings from well outside the colony.

Do not stand for lengthy periods right in front of or close to cave entrances, mines, culverts or cliffs, or sandy banks. Breeding, sometimes roosting swiftlets, kingfishers, bee-eaters, pardalotes, martins, swallows, and so on, will be trying to enter caves, cavities, overhangs or burrows.

Photography at nests used to be very popular. Now it is considered rather a passive type of photography and the 'action photo' showing bird behaviour, taken with a long lens, either hand-held or on a tripod, is considered *de rigueur*. We broadly agree with that.

Never modify vegetation about a nest for the sake of a photo. There have been many shocking incidents over the years, where vegetation that concealed a nest has been cut back, often with saws, hedge clippers or secateurs, to enable a photographer to get a clear view. Bush bird nests have been pulled out of their original location, and then set up lower down, to get 'that picture'. Hollow tree limbs have been sawn or chopped open. Clods of clay or earth have been stuffed into burrow entrances to prevent small birds such as Rainbow Bee-eaters, pardalotes, martins, or White-backed Swallows from entering. Then the clod has been forgotten and the baby birds inside have died.

Some humans are feral in behaviour and should not be carelessly guided to nests. Do not show nests to anybody or tell them the location. Smuggling is rife in our region. It is in the breeding season that such activities come to a head.

If you see a suspicious person or activity in your travels, take vehicle registration numbers when possible but look very seriously indeed to your own safety. Do not, under any circumstances, approach people you feel may be engaged in underhand

Crimson Chat. Here is a fledgling, just a little more advanced than the Southern Scrub-robin on page 143. The tail feathers in their covering sheaths are erupting. The black mark on the crown is a shadow! The bird is out of the nest, may be able to fly but is a dependent bird still. Larapinta Trail, Western MacDonnell Ranges, Northern Territory

work. Observe without being seen and slip away quietly. Report suspicious activity to senior police, senior rangers, tribal leaders or other recognised public figures. Insist on a receipt for any written, photographic or other evidence you hand over. Ideally, go accompanied by a solicitor or with a witness, to make formal statements or hand over evidence. And don't delay. If poachers can be caught red-handed, so much the better.

Damaged nests

Can you repair a damaged nest? Under a *few* circumstances interference with a nesting site (that is, rescue of it) is warranted. We have already mentioned collapsed bird burrows. A common 'bird nest disaster' is for a nest to be blown out of a tree or bush during strong winds. Ideally, you should replace the nest *exactly* where it came from. A more usual but less satisfactory result is to place the nest as far up the tree as you can, and if done quickly enough, the parents may resume their nest duties.

Ken once stuffed a fallen Noisy Miner's nest containing three small nestlings into an old black plastic flowerpot. It was then wired to a horizontal bough three metres from the ground. The parents (and helpers) returned within minutes and successfully reared the chicks to fledging stage over the next week. Plastic flowerpots make good temporary nests because of the assorted sizes available, and you can readily cut them to a new shape if need be. Black or green are best; orange, yellow, red or blue flowerpots just don't look so good in a tree.

If you find a fully fledged young bird alone on the ground, don't assume it has been abandoned. It may be just out of the nest and not so good at flying yet. Move the fledgling only if it is in urgent danger. The parents are probably watching, and if you interfere too much, they will abandon it. It is better to ask a wildlife rescue service for advice than to 'rescue' young birds on your own.

Artificial nests

Some birds make use of the built environment to assist their breeding efforts, a good example being the House Sparrow. The adaptability of some species has encouraged experiments in providing artificial nests when suitable tree hollows are lacking. This practice is not always the solution it seems, as adaptable species such as mynas make enthusiastic use of artificial nest hollows intended for lorikeets and parrots. BOCA has information on recommended box sizes and advice on siting them, but if you install artificial nest hollows in your garden or local park, *you* are the one who must take responsibility for protecting them from unwanted lodgers.

Try to fix boxes where they cannot be reached by foxes, cats, rats or children. Snakes cannot easily be kept out, nor can goannas. Occasionally, small mammals may move in: small bats *Antechinus*, Feather-tailed, Sugar or Squirrel Gliders, or native rodents. You may end up with Brush-tailed or Ring-tailed Possums.

Sexual dimorphism again. A pair of adult Painted Firetails, female at left. Kings Canyon, Northern Territory

In a blur of movement, an adult Welcome Swallow (at left), feeds one of its nestlings. These young are well on the way to being fully fledged, with most of the feathers of their first plumage evident. The duller plumage and pale cream gape skin will persist for several weeks. The young will still be dependent for a while before they become free-flying. Cobungra, Victorian Alps

Feral bees and European wasps are a problem and should be instantly removed by fumigation. The box should then be thoroughly cleaned and left open to the weather for at least twelve months before further use.

Wire baskets of varying shapes and sizes, hung in trees or under a wide verandah, may attract birds, which might use them as a base for their own nest. A tiny shelf or bracket twelve centimetres (five inches) below the ceiling in a sheltered alcove of an outbuilding or barn may encourage Welcome Swallows to build a mud nest. A second shelf below, to catch the swallow droppings, is recommended.

In Australia's wet tropics, many houses have a Olive-backed Sunbird's nest hanging from a hook, light-fitting, or wandering vine. Australasian Gannets are breeding on old navigation beacons in Port Phillip Bay, Victoria, along with our personal pride and joy—one solitary Cape Gannet (the South African species, a vagrant) which has paired with a local bird and now produces a hybrid youngster each year.

Beware of the imported 'bird houses' and silly little feeders that are increasingly coming on to the market. They suit American and European birds and will increase your garden population of introduced sparrows, mynas and turtle-doves, while doing nothing at all for Australasian species.

CHAPTER TEN

Seasonal routines

In Chapter Seven, we looked at the daily routines and regular behaviour of birds. On a much broader time scale, birds also have a range of seasonal behaviours of interest to birdwatchers.

Moulting

All birds moult at least once a year, to renew their feathers. Some moult twice or even three times a year. Traditionally, moulting is thought of as 'pre-nuptial', when male birds may assume bright feathers or extra plumes for courtship; or 'post-breeding', a more complete moult to replace worn and damaged feathers. Immature birds will moult and gain the next year's plumage, perhaps markedly different from the one they are shedding. These descriptions are more suited to the temperate zones of the world. In the tropics and arid zones, food and water supplies are less regulated and annual moults and breeding cycles may sometimes coincide.

Birds that depend on flight for feeding moult gradually, but many waterbirds (some ducks, swans, grebes) shed all their flight feathers simultaneously. They may move to large lakes or the coast, where they are safer from predators.

Waterfowl such as the Australian Shelduck assemble in large flocks in southern Victoria at the Western Sewage Treatment Works. The shelducks lose their flight feathers (primaries) all at once and for several weeks they are then confined to the wider, deeper sewage ponds, keeping away from foxes and rather vulnerable to prowling Swamp Harriers. When disturbed, they splash away across the water, thrashing wildly.

Penguins have one annual moult and must leave the water to undertake it. Each year, having eaten as much food as possible, they come ashore at the appointed time, stand around for two to three weeks or so, initially becoming dreadfully tatty, then starting to improve in appearance as the new feathers finally push out all of the old ones. Immature penguins usually moult a little earlier than the adult birds. Adult penguins moult when their breeding season is over. Only when they have a complete suit again, oiled and sleek, can they safely re-enter the water. To get by during the moult they fast, using the stored body fats for nutrition and for the formation of the

Male Variegated Fairy-wren beginning to resume its breeding plumage.
Such changeling birds can look very 'patchy'. Mungo National Park,
New South Wales

new feathers. Woe betide a penguin that was unable to lay down a good fat deposit—
it could be starving and weakened at the end of the moult.

Please do not disturb any moulting penguins you may locate along a beach. These
birds are extremely vulnerable to predators at this time. View them from a distance
that is sufficient to cause no stress. If one of the penguins is any other than your own
locally breeding species, then photograph or draw the salient features if you can and
report them to the nearest conservation ranger or wildlife expert. Record the date and
place, your name, and any other details you can discern of the penguin's behaviour
and condition. If you want to help the birds, mount a discreet guard, to keep people,
dogs and dune buggies away.

Most songbirds moult wing and body feathers progressively over a number of
months. Any large birds flying above you can be scrutinised for wing and tail feather
loss. When ravens, crows or Rooks call overhead, look for the slots in the wings where
opposite pairs of feathers seem to fall together. How symmetrical is the feather loss?

Think about the fairy-wrens for a moment. After breeding, most of the males suddenly become patchy and lose their bright colours, with only the tail colour as a clue
to sex. In the spring, the dominant male of each family gradually blossoms into the
little gem we know so well. They look very interesting as they make the colour
changes, so try to make a special effort to see them. Occasionally a mature, dominant
male fairy-wren will retain his bright colours through the winter.

Moulted feathers

In late summer, autumn and early winter, you can expect to find interesting feathers lying about the landscape. Sometimes a moulted feather on the ground is the only evidence you will get of the recent presence of a bird. Collecting feathers and having them in your possession is illegal but you should certainly examine and perhaps draw or photograph what you have found. Peter Roger's lovely photo of a moulted crest feather (see page 2), unmistakably that of a Sulphur-crested Cockatoo, is a perfect example.

You can become a skilled feather detective if you make a point of inspecting and analysing every feather you find in the bush, by a lake or along the shore. Which species does it come from? Which part of the bird does it represent? Is it a tail feather or a wing feather? Which side of the body does it come from? How old was the bird that dropped it? Is the feather showing signs of wear? Many birds slowly wear away the tips of their tails, leaving a ragged, dilapidated edge. The longer the period since the last moult, the untidier wing and tail tips may become. Birds which forage on or close to the ground, or which habitually climb tree trunks, often show extreme examples of this.

If you find yourself near a flock of moulting birds (various waterfowl, Eurasian Coot, perhaps gulls), you can look at many dropped feathers. Mentally fit them to different parts of the bird. Again, look for feathers from left and right sides. Don't let the chance for extra study go by!

Migration

Many birds are not year-round residents of any one area. For a variety of reasons, birds may move about the landscape.

Migration is a regular movement around parts of the globe to take advantage of areas with the best food supply. Migration is risky, requiring much energy. Many birds are lost when winds blow them off course or they arrive at their destination to find conditions at their traditional feeding grounds changed.

Some of these birds are highly tuned to precise arrival and departure dates. They nest, raise young, enter post-breeding moults and leave breeding areas in the same synchronised timetable each year.

Why do some birds travel so far?

There is no single, satisfactory explanation for this behaviour. It *may* be to do with the continuing slow movements of the continental masses over millions of years. It is certainly related to long-term weather patterns.

What is also known is that birds breeding in, say, the Arctic Circle, tend to move to the other end of the earth, the Antarctic Circle, if possible. The distribution of southern land masses doesn't quite permit most of them to go all the way, so they settle for what they can get—in our case Australia and New Zealand. The Arctic Tern *can* go all the way and stays at sea, feeding along the edge of the southern pack ice.

By contrast, birds from our northern tropics tend to make a shorter migration into similar tropical regions across the Equator. The distances travelled northward roughly match the distance of the return southward journey.

Routes taken by migrating birds

Many birds cross over Bass Strait from Tasmania to Victoria and South Australia. Birds travel up the Great Dividing Range, along the coast of Australia, and offshore along the Great Barrier Reef. Birds almost certainly arrive and leave northern Australia through Cape York Peninsula, or Arnhem Land or from the Kimberley, and from North Cape in New Zealand. Birds cross Cook Strait between New Zealand's North and South Islands, or Foveaux Strait further south. Seabirds also move up and down the edges of the continental shelves of both Australia and New Zealand.

Autumn and spring observations, in a locality you know well, may establish which species are moving through.

East–west international migrants

New Zealand's Banded Dotterel (our Double-banded Plover) is a summer breeder in the Land of the Long White Cloud, and many of them migrate to winter quarters on the South Island, or to Australia, spreading themselves from Perth in Western

Australia all the way around the coastal zone to about Bundaberg in Queensland. In eclipse plumage (another name for non-breeding plumage) they often join flocks of Northern Hemisphere waders and have to be sorted out by birdwatchers.

Other east–west wintering migrants from New Zealand to Australia are the Fluttering and Hutton's Shearwaters, a reasonable proportion of the juvenile population of the Australasian Gannet, and the White-fronted Tern. Some Shining Bronze-Cuckoos come to Australia, too.

The Cattle Egret has become an easily observable example of a true annual migration, one which is a fairly recent phenomenon within Australasia.

The rufous flanks show this to be the Tasmanian migrant race of the Silvereye. Photographed during northward migration in March. Licola, Victoria

CATTLE EGRETS

During winter in south-eastern and south-western Australia and Tasmania, keep an eye out for herds of cattle, usually dairy cows, with an accompanying group of white Cattle Egrets in close attendance. The birds are stocky, hunched and heron-shaped, with long slender necks, stand over half a metre high on dark legs and have long yellow-orange pointed beaks. At the onset of winter, these egrets arrive in southern Australia from their wetland breeding colonies in New South Wales and southern coastal Queensland (breeding colonies also extend right across northern Australia to the Wyndham region).

There were tentative introductions and some probable wild bird sightings from 1933 onward, but the dramatic spread of this bird across Australia began in earnest in the late forties and early fifties.

The Cattle Egret is said to have a self-beneficial (one-way or commensal) relationship with the cattle. They eat creatures disturbed as the cattle graze. Perhaps they also eat seeds from dung, or churned mud. The cattle do not receive any obvious benefit from the egrets, except for the indirect one of having their feeding areas largely 'cleaned' of pests.

Another well-known Australian bird species with a similar relationship to stock is the diminutive Willie Wagtail. We frequently see them riding on the backs of cows or horses, or prancing about so close to the noses of the large animals that the birds are occasionally blown away by an annoyed snort. The introduced but unloved Common Myna is also a commensal species with stock.

Cattle Egrets are considered a boon to agriculture, and, like the occasional flocks of Australian White and Straw-necked Ibis, are a winter-long presence, helping to free pastures of generally unwanted invertebrates.

From September to November, the crowns, necks, chests and upper backs of the Cattle Egret become a rich rufous, almost tan-orange. This is the onset of the breeding plumage of the adults and simultaneously you will realise that their numbers are dropping. Soon only a small number of plain white ones will be left. These, the last to go, may be the immature or younger birds, but some will breed in their first season of migration northward. The southern paddocks will be devoid of Cattle Egrets in summer until the following autumn when they all come back again. Watch for them. Observers living in central and eastern New South Wales may see them travelling north or south in the early summer and late autumn.

If you live in New Zealand you will have learned that the Cattle Egrets first arrived in 1963. That's the official time, anyway (Thursday morning, half-past ten?); there were probably a few before that. The flocks built up annually, and quite large numbers are now present in the winter months. They favour farmland and are found in both islands. But they all return to eastern Australia, to New South Wales and Queensland, for the summer breeding season.

The Cattle Egret has also become an annual east–west migrant, another trans-Tasman species. Perhaps one day they will decide that they can breed in New Zealand and no longer need to migrate across the sea.

South–north international migrants

A few bird species breed in the Southern Hemisphere during our summer season, then go north across the Equator for the winter. They include several petrels, the Short-tailed and Sooty Shearwaters being the best known. The White-faced Storm-Petrel (Takahikare-moana) is included. Some from Australia go to the Indian Ocean, but the whereabouts of many in the non-breeding season is unknown. Some from New Zealand may go north-east into the tropical Pacific Ocean. Wilson's Storm-Petrel and also the South Polar Skua travel far north from the Antarctic.

Many seabirds move northward to escape the Antarctic winter, spending the season in southern temperate regions or less rigorous pelagic areas north of the Antarctic Circle. Some are seen around Australasia's southern shores: albatrosses, giant-petrels, many other petrels, Great Skua. The migratory penguins seem to spread themselves out in the oceanic mass to our south, with only occasional stragglers reaching our shoreline.

Some birds routinely move in and out of Australia, travelling into New Guinea and sometimes on to Indonesia and other areas of South-East Asia. One of these is the Australian Pratincole. Pratincoles are now known to be closely allied to the terns and are certainly tern-like in flight.

Several bronze-cuckoo species from southern Australia, as well as the Common Koel and Channel-billed Cuckoo from eastern and northern Australia, all move north to winter in various areas of New Guinea and Indonesia.

Some of New Zealand's Shining Bronze-Cuckoo population crosses into north-eastern Queensland and may travel on northward, too. The Long-tailed Cuckoo of New Zealand travels north into the tropical islands, ranging from Raoul Island to many islands of the western Pacific Ocean.

Amongst the cuckoo-shrikes and trillers, several are 'partial international migrants', in that *some* wintering birds cross into parts of New Guinea, the Solomon Islands and Indonesia. Some wintering Tree Martins also move north to destinations north of Australia. The list of such species is quite long.

North–south international migrants

The White-winged Black Tern flies in from Eurasian and South-East Asian regions to spend the summer in Australia and New Zealand. So does the Oriental Pratincole, occasionally arriving in thousands in northern Australia.

Breeding only in the far north of the Northern Hemisphere, the Arctic, Pomarine and Long-tailed Jaegers, also the Arctic Tern, undertake an annual migration southward to escape the Arctic cold. The Oriental Cuckoo and two large swifts, the White-throated Needletail and Fork-tailed Swift, also come to our region from north-eastern Asia. All three of the latter turn up in New Zealand as summer stragglers, the cuckoo less often.

A dark morph of the Southern Giant-Petrel incubating on a nest in the lee of rocks, Stilbocarpa and peat. This is a pelagic petrel that returns to sub-Antarctic islands to breed. Aurora Point, Macquarie Island

Waders

Within Australasia, ten families comprise 'the waders' (shorebirds)—a collective term. Like the raptors, waders can become an obsession for some observers. Many waders breed in the Northern Hemisphere and fly to the Southern Hemisphere for our summer. They are generally birds of seashores and tidal inlets, but may also break their journeys on salt lakes and other wetlands far from the coast. As an example, recently created sewage ponds at Alice Springs in central Australia have become an important wader stopover point.

It is a fact of life that the north–south waders visit us each year. The trick is to identify each species accurately. In the Northern Hemisphere the annual migrant waders are mostly in their distinctive breeding plumages. Thus they are relatively easy to identify correctly. The challenge for bird observers 'downunder' is that the waders mostly arrive wearing their non-breeding (eclipse) plumage. This means that identification of some species relies on such subtleties as leg and toe colour or comparative bill length. We have previously spoken of 'LBJs' (little brown jobs) amongst the small bush birds. You may feel that 'CGJ'—'confusing grey jobs'—is more useful to describe many waders. Most of the expert wader watchers that we know are blessed with long sight. If you want to become a serious wader watcher, you will eventually feel the need to purchase a telescope.

Snipe, godwits, curlews, sandpipers and other Scolopacidae

Is it easier to identify waders by family appearance or by behaviour? Well, it depends on which family we choose. Snipe, godwits, curlews and sandpipers are members of the most complicated wader family, the Scolopacidae. Their size varies. It is useful to divide them up by their habitat preferences and manner of feeding, as they often congregate in mixed groups and to the beginner many of the smaller ones look very much alike, with greyish-brown patterned backs (particularly in non-breeding plumage) and white underbellies. Most of these birds are annual north–south migrants. We will look at a selection of them; remember, we are now discussing behaviour as well as appearance.

Snipe are more compact than godwits, but have very long straight bills and larger eyes. They tend to hide in dense cover in moist vegetation and are often seen only when flushed. These surely are amongst the more difficult waders to see adequately.

Godwits have long bills which in some species turn slightly up at the end (male and female bills vary in length). They feed in flocks on tidal flats, and may 'walk around their bill' to probe deeper into sand. Knots are plumper, shorter billed, but often feed with godwits, and have the same probing method of obtaining food. Practise sorting out Red Knots from Great Knots.

The Eastern Curlew has a very distinctive call. Its bill can be five times as long as its head. The curlews and whimbrels with their long, down-curved beaks, are fairly easy to identify as long as you learn the body-size, height and stance differences, and degree of bill curvature. Just the same, making decisions on identity between Whimbrels and Little Curlews out there on the shimmering mudflats is *not* always easy.

This Grey Teal, a nomad, is performing a wing-comfort stretch, beautifully displaying the wing feather anatomy, including the metallic green, reflective speculum. Serendip Sanctuary, Victoria

The short-legged, dark-chested Ruddy Turnstones are busy feeders, turning over shells, seaweed and beach litter as they search for food. Look for them mostly on rocky shores, reefs and headlands.

Sandpipers mostly feed on mudflats or the shallow edges of wetlands, pushing their slim bills deep into sand or soft mud. The sparrow-sized stints are also of the sandpiper group (all are 'CGJs' incarnate). Greenshanks have similar feeding methods and may also run briskly after small fish. Yellowlegs snatch invertebrates from the surface of the water. Tattlers are likely to be seen in any coastal habitat. Phalaropes spin in circles to stir invertebrates to the water surface. They are rare migrants.

An adult Black-fronted Dotterel, a nomadic bird
favouring freshwater wetlands.

Plovers and dotterels, the family Charadriidae

There are international migrants amongst these Charadriidae, too. Lesser and Greater Sand Plovers, the rare Oriental and Caspian Plovers, the Ringed and Little Ringed Plovers are all in this category. Of the Northern Hemisphere migrants wintering (that is, spending their winter, our summer) in Australasia, the Pacific Golden Plover and the Grey Plover are probably the 'flag carriers' of the family.

We have previously mentioned the Double-banded Plover (Tuturiwhatu), a trans-Tasman migrant. Wrybills migrate only *within* New Zealand.

Nomads amongst the local waders

Not all members of the wader families are annual international migrants.

Within Australia, several members of the plover–dotterel family Charadriidae can be migrants *or* nomads (almost at will, it would appear). These are the widespread Red-capped Plover, the ocean beach-dwelling Hooded Plover, the Red-kneed and Black-fronted Dotterels (which prefer fresh water), the Shore Plover of South East Island in the Chathams, and the New Zealand Dotterel (also called Tuturiwhatu). The dotterels and small plovers run rapidly in spurts, their little legs 'twinkling' in a most characteristic way.

Banded and Masked Lapwings are nomadic and can sometimes be seen in large flocks. The Masked Lapwing has two forms, the northern with longer facial wattles, and the southern 'Spur-winged Plover'. The smaller Banded Lapwing is often found far from water on the open plains.

The locally nomadic to sedentary Bush Stone-curlew (family Burhinidae) and highly nomadic Inland Dotterel (family Charadriidae) are waders that have adapted to life away from the sea. There is also the strange Painted Snipe (family Rostratulidae), a world-wide species, but the Australian subspecies has become relatively rare.

Let's move on to two more families that are nomadic rather than migratory.

Oystercatchers (family Haematopodidae) are robust black, white, or pied coastal waders with red eyes and red blade-like bills that are flattened from the side to enable them to poke into shells or prise their food from rocks. They are striking to look at, and very photogenic when seen against grey rocks or pale sand. Once you have identified your first oystercatcher you will have no trouble in recognising the rest of the family. There are two, the Pied and the Sooty, in Australia; and three, the South Island Pied Oystercatcher, the Variable Oystercatcher (Torea), and the Chatham Island Oystercatcher, in New Zealand. Oystercatchers take several years to reach maturity, and then mate for life.

Stilts and avocets (family Recurvirostridae) have very long thin legs for their height, so long that these limbs trail behind in flight. Stilts have long fine bills. Avocets' bills are even longer, and elegantly curved upward at the end (hence their generic name, *Recurvirostra* or curved-billed). Sadly, New Zealand's Black Stilt (Kaki), a bird of the braided river beds of the South Island, is becoming rare. The Banded

Stilt appears to be a partial migrant within Australia in that many assemble to bree at inland salt lakes in some years but are nomadic the rest of the time.

Within each of these two families (oystercatchers, and stilts and avocets) the members have a similar body shape, but can be readily identified by their colour differences.

Sedentary waders

New Zealand has two species of endemic, non-migratory snipe, the New Zealand Snipe—sometimes called Sub-Antarctic Snipe—and the Chatham Island Snipe. Both are members of the Scolopacidae. The relatively sedentary Plains-wanderer (family Pedionomidae) is becoming rare, a legacy of ever-increasing land clearance and predation. Specialist tours can be undertaken to see this species in central southern New South Wales.

The wonderful Beach Stone-curlew is relatively sedentary in its tropical coastal range. The Comb-crested Jacana or Lilytrotter of warmer wetlands in Australia is considered sedentary. This is the bird with the really long thin toes that you see walking on wide floating waterlily leaves and similar vegetation.

HOW TO RECORD MIGRATION IN ACTION

You can record bird species and numbers regularly throughout the year. Enter the results on a chart to display the arrivals and departures of species in your region. Over several years, you will begin to have a *most* imposing chart behind the loo door.

- Go to a prominent headland along the coast and record all seabird species you see, as well as the numbers, four times in a year as a minimum. Go weekly or monthly if you can. Record as above. Keep seabird records on a chart behind the laundry door.
- Go to a known shearwater (muttonbird) colony in midwinter. It is a sad, empty place. Go more often as spring approaches. One evening, the place will be alive with birds—they are back!
- On the same theme, go again to your muttonbird colony in the dusk and just before dawn in fine, clear late spring to early summer weather. *Don't get too close* but sit back and enjoy the arrivals and departures.
- Each year, look for late summer and early autumn flocks or concentrations of known migratory birds in the countryside near your home. Examples may be various seabirds, Cattle Egret, waders, Swift and Orange-bellied Parrots, various cuckoos, swifts, Dollarbird, Rainbow Bee-eater, Striated Pardalote, some honeyeaters, Flame Robin, Black-faced Cuckoo-shrike, Olive-backed Oriole, swallows and martins, Clamorous Reed-Warbler, Tasmanian subspecies of the Silvereye.

Stragglers, vagrants and strays

Birds often go the 'wrong way', are blown off-course by cyclones and strong storm fronts, are caught up with 'exuberant' flocks of related or even entirely different species, or are genuine, wilful explorers and colonisers. Some may settle some-where part of the way through a migratory or nomadic flight. Others may wander further than normal because of drought, fire or flood in the region from which they came.

All birdwatchers hope to see a rare bird now and then, but some people make it an art form. It is often twitchers who find vagrant birds. They pursue reported sightings with gusto. Twitchers like to go birding in far-flung places, continental shelves and offshore islands, remote desert centres, and almost impenetrable rainforests. If they can find something 'new' for the country, so much the better.

Protection for international migrant birds

After a major conference in 1971, in a small town named Ramsar in Iran, eighteen nations established a worldwide system for cataloguing and protecting important feeding grounds for international migratory birds. The *Convention on Wetlands of International Importance* is now commonly referred to as the Ramsar Convention and there are currently over eighty countries involved. The protected places, known as 'Ramsar sites', offer safe havens for local and travelling migratory birds. More are needed. They are supposed to be inviolate from interference or development, and governments have contracted to protect them. But, of course, it doesn't always work that way and the system is continually under challenge.

Other international treaties are in place, such as JAMBA and CAMBA, which stand for Japan–Australia and China–Australia Migratory Bird Agreements respectively. They are supposed to protect the birds travelling between those countries.

Altitudinal migration

Birds that live, frequently breeding, in mountain country, and come down from winter cold and snow to the hinterland or coastal plains below are known to be engaged in altitudinal migration. In most cases only part of the population shifts, not the whole. In south-eastern Australia such birds include Yellow-tailed Black-Cockatoo, Gang-gang Cockatoo, Australian King-Parrot, Crimson Rosella, Flame Robin, perhaps Pink and Rose Robins, Rufous Fantail, Pied Currawong.

Winter flocks

Vast numbers of waterfowl of many species form winter flocks in many parts of our region. One of the autumn and winter features of the Western Sewage Treatment Works ('The Farm', as it has long been known) outside Melbourne is the sight of at least eight thousand Pink-eared Ducks flying in black masses against the sky, all whistling loudly. Swamp Harriers are the usual culprits in putting the resting or feeding flocks to flight. Hundreds of Blue-billed Ducks and several thousand Hoary-headed Grebes assemble there at times.

Masked Lapwings assemble in wintering flocks in some districts, although these may be loosely scattered over a large region. We have seen such flocks at Kakadu National Park in the Northern Territory, at Phillip Island in Victoria, and in Tasmania. Flocks also gather here and there in New Zealand, and are thought to be non-breeders and juveniles.

Another species that concentrates very markedly in the winter months is the Magpie-lark, now classified as a monarch flycatcher. Flocks may be scattered over a wide area, but are unmistakable when found. Recently Ken saw a flock of several hundred on powerlines along a busy highway on the outskirts of Townsville, Queensland.

Australian Magpies, outside the territorial pairs or families that maintain their own territory, are frequently chivvied from one territory to another in winter until they reach common ground where no territory exists. We could call this a 'wintering ground' if it is in the winter months. Driving a country highway or secondary road, you might discover several dozen Australian Magpies scattered all over a wide, open paddock. There may be ravens amongst them. If the flock persists into the early summer, as it often does, it may be regarded as a non-breeders' ground. Most of the birds will be comparatively young, but the few that are older may well be those that have lost mates or are currently single for one reason or another.

Without going too close, observe Australian Magpie or Magpie-lark flocks such as these to ascertain the relative proportions of males, females and immature birds. Keep the records from year to year. Record the locality and dates as well.

Mixed-species flocks

A lovely phenomenon of the bush, occurring in both Australia and New Zealand and elsewhere, is the association of mixed-species flocks. Soon after the breeding seasons of the small and medium-sized bush birds, many gather in often quite large aggre-

gations, and move through a tract of country that we could call their 'collective home range'. This is often a mid-summer to autumn occurrence and may persist all winter in some areas, until pairing off for breeding begins.

The whole group may travel around its range several times daily and the composition of the flock may vary from day to day. Mostly, insectivorous species are involved. The birds forage at every height, from ground litter to the top of tree canopies, and benefit from the protection of a large flock. Early in the season juvenile birds are often in tow, still partly dependent on their parents. A cuckoo or two

Male Flame Robin standing on seaweed on a beach.
This is a wintering altitudinal migrant species in eastern Australia.
Whisky Bay, Wilsons Promontory, Victoria

may also be present. Such flocks, in southern Australia, invariably have thornbills as a core species.

In inland northern Queensland, centring on Charters Towers, a study based on one hundred and twenty-seven mixed flocks found that twelve species frequently present could be called 'core species', and another twelve or so variously joined in. The top eight in order were Willie Wagtail, Striated Pardalote, Rufous Whistler, Weebill, Yellow-rumped Thornbill, Black-faced Woodswallow, Singing Honeyeater and Double-barred Finch.

The numbers in some mixed flocks in northern Australia can be so large that observers refer to a 'wave'. One, in the Kimberley District in north-western Australia, near the Old Beverley Springs Station in May 1979 (the dry season), numbered in 'hundreds if not thousands'. The first eight species (and presumably the highest numbers in sequence) were White-winged Triller, Black-faced Woodswallow, Varied Lorikeet, Weebill, Yellow-tinted Honeyeater, Jacky Winter, Banded Honeyeater and Little Friarbird. At least another six species were involved.

In a mixed flock in south Western Australia in 1949, the six dominant species recorded were White-winged Triller, Black-faced Woodswallow, Jacky Winter, Weebill, Willie Wagtail and Varied Sittella.

In New Zealand, Yellowheads often follow groups of Kakariki (the parakeets), and a few other species may join in. Saddlebacks seem to attract Fantails and Whiteheads, which accompany the larger birds and forage about them.

Flocks like this can enliven a day's birdwatching and provide a bonanza of different species. Look for such flocks in your local parkland and bush reserves. Record their composition and their daily movements, if you can.

Nomadic flocks

Many species may pass through your district in flocks, moving between feeding grounds or in response to seasonal stimuli. Look for ducks, magpie-geese, grebes, herons, night herons, fruit pigeons, lorikeets, Cockatiels, woodswallows, many honeyeaters, silvereyes and starlings.

FLOCK AND COLLECTIVE NAMES

Ducks on the edge of a waterhole or on an island in a swamp are said to be 'loafing'. A 'camp' of ducks is sometimes used for whistling-ducks. Waders clustered on a sandbar or rocky headland at high tide are 'roosting' or 'at a tidal roost'.

Well-known examples of antique group names for some birds: a skein of geese, a wisp of snipe, a murder of crows, a charm of goldfinches, a wing of plovers, an unkindness of ravens.

PART FOUR:

Your birdwatching kit

A little tent as a hide. An early morning visit by a Malleefowl brightens one's day. Little Desert National Park, western Victoria

Adult Crimson Rosella.
Tidal River, Victoria

CHAPTER ELEVEN

In the field

Birdwatching can be as cheap or as expensive a hobby as you wish. It requires a minimum of special tools (binoculars, a field guide, a notebook) and provides an introduction to the natural world, at any age and with any level of fitness. The optional expenses are special clothing, subscriptions, reference books and journals, a telescope, a camera, and video and travel costs.

This chapter deals with the basic 'what', 'where' and 'how' of birdwatching, as well as some opportunities for learning more.

Birdwatching equipment

Binoculars

Binoculars (field glasses) are nigh-on essential for birdwatchers. You *can* be a birdwatcher without binoculars, but if you choose *not* to own them, you will be confining yourself to watching large species and those that happen to stray close to you. We bet you will want to get a pair in the end.

When it comes to deciding *which* binoculars to buy, we enter a minefield of personal likes and dislikes, delights and disappointments. So, what to do? You might ask other birdwatchers. If you belong to a birdwatching organisation you can ring them for advice. Then go to an optical instruments store or major camera retailer and look at the wide range of brands available. It is possible to spend several thousand dollars for a top-quality pair of binoculars, but if you are just starting out on a new hobby you need to be very sure they are suited to your needs. The cheapest models may distort colours, and can't always be mended if you drop them. It might be better to buy something more moderately priced. When you have more experience you will be able to judge your own requirements.

An alternative is to borrow binoculars for the first few weeks. Many families own a pair which were previously used in the army, at the races, or on the sea. Some of these will be very heavy compared with modern designs.

You will hear people talking about their binoculars, saying 'I prefer eight forties for the bush, and a pair of ten fifties for the birds over the sea.' Somebody may respond 'Yes, but since I do most of my birding in dense bush, I prefer seven

Waterbirds camped at wetlands and photographed with a normal (50-millimetre) lens. A nice rural scene with birds. Near Glen Innes, northern New South Wales

thirties for really close work, and they're small enough to be shoved in a pocket if it rains. Mind you, I've got Dad's old army sixteen fifties for the waders if I ever want to go to the coast.'

What are they talking about? 'Eight forties' first refers to the *magnification* of the lenses (eight times the image), and then to the *width* of the front lenses, where the light enters. Forty is the number of millimetres across that leading lens.

Examine a standard pair of binoculars closely, and somewhere on the body will be engraved the legend '7 x 35' or '8 x 40' or '10 x 50' or even '16 x 50'. The more compact models may be '7 x 30' or '8 x 30' or '10 x 25'.

Magnification is the number of times that the binoculars actually multiply the size of the target image (usually 7, 8, 10 or 16 times). Should you go for magnifications above ten, it becomes more difficult to focus steadily on your target. Everything is magnified, including the slight shake of your hands and the movement caused by wind blowing across the binoculars. Also, the field of view will decrease with greater magnification. This means that if your distant bird moves only a few metres you may temporarily lose it. Heat haze, smoke, spray or fog will also work against you.

Width is the diameter of the front (objective) lens. If you divide the objective lens by the magnification you obtain the 'light factor', which tells you the light-gathering power of the lens. '7 x 35' has a light factor of five, as do '8 x 40' and '10 x 50'. This is the minimum you will be happy with for birdwatching in most conditions. If you spend a lot of time in shady bushland, you may even choose a '7 x 50', with a light factor of seven. The compact models such as 8 x 30 have a light factor of less than four, and the 10 x 25 only two and a half.

Anyone with arthritis in the hands, or a painful condition of the neck, shoulders or lower spine, will be unable to hold heavy binoculars up to their eyes for long. It is possible to buy some really tiny binoculars; but whilst the magnification is good, their field of view is usually narrow. If weight is a major consideration, look for the very best quality you can afford in the compact sizes. These will provide the best compromise between weight, optical quality, and ease of use.

Field of view does not depend on the width of the objective lens, but on the internal construction of the lenses. 'Wide angle' binoculars are the best for birdwatching as you don't have to re-focus so often to follow the bird's movements, but beware the sales pitch. One brand's 'wide angle' is another's standard lens.

Binoculars that come with 'automatic zoom' lenses are not generally recommended for birdwatching.

If you usually go birding in extreme weather conditions, whether hot, cold or steamy, you will need to take that into consideration and probably pay a little more for sealed lenses.

Buying binoculars cannot be rushed. Get a pair that you feel really comfortable with. Spend time trying out several shapes and sizes. The different makes and

What a difference a lens makes. Part of the same group taken without moving any human feet. Now we can see Australian White Ibis, many Royal Spoonbills and some Pacific Black Duck. Photographed with a 300-millimetre telephoto lens. The effect is comparable to using your normal eyesight and then switching to 10 x 50 binoculars. Near Glen Innes, northern New South Wales

models are suited to different face and hand proportion. Some may be too big for you to wrap your hands around. Your hands need to fall naturally onto the focus wheel or knurl so that you can make the constant fine adjustments needed in the field. Width between the eyes is very variable, and although any good binoculars can be adjusted, some may never feel quite right. If you continually have to adjust for black areas in front of your eyes, the proportions aren't right for your face.

If you wear spectacles, buy binoculars with eye-piece rubbers that fold back out of the way, so that the lens is closer to your spectacle lens. Some binoculars have longer eye pieces and these are useful if you have a tendency to hold the binoculars away from your face (perhaps because you have long eyelashes!). You need to keep the rubbers extended to cut out light from the side.

When birdwatching, always keep your binocular strap around your neck. Shoulder and back harnesses can be obtained for greater comfort. If you are going to be out all day, then something that reduces drag on your neck muscles is surely a boon.

Cold weather, cold mornings, hot weather, hot humid mornings, can create problems. In cold weather the warmth of your body will fog up the glasses, so keep them in the warm interior of the car when travelling. In hot weather, if travelling with the air-conditioning on, carry the binoculars, telescope and cameras in the boot, where they will be closer to the external temperature and more effective on arrival. Only if you are actively birdwatching along the way should they be inside with you.

Your binoculars are a finely tuned instrument; treat them with respect. In a vehicle, we always place the binoculars on the floor. That way, they cannot fall off the seat, and only a real calamity will damage them.

Telescopes

Telescopes are useful for distant waders and other shy birds, but have all the disadvantages of strong magnification. They work best in good light conditions, and since the field of view is so concentrated, lining up your bird takes a little practice.

Selecting and purchasing a telescope (spotting-scope) is much the same as for binoculars. Some are virtually fixed lenses with a focus wheel, others have zoom lenses as well. The choice is wide and the prices usually range from high to steep. There is no doubt that some of them are magnificent instruments. With the telescope you also *have* to buy a good strong tripod, an extra but compulsory and also expensive investment.

Field guide

A proper field guide is a series of coloured paintings and descriptive text, ordered in a way that demonstrates relationships of some kind between species. Its purpose is to assist in identification, but it is only a 'guide'. Each one differs slightly in content and approach to field identification.

Why do genuine field guides not contain photographs? Because living creatures such as birds have more interest in concealing their identity from us than in adopting artificial poses which display all their identifying marks at the same time.

Bird Observers Club of Australia members with telescopes line the edge of a sewage pond to identify waders. Western Treatment Plant, Werribee, Victoria

Photographs of living birds vary immeasurably in the amount of detail that they provide. Light, film quality and development and printing variations may distort colour. Photographic anthologies are a very useful adjunct to field guides with painted images, but cannot really replace them.

Field guides are illustrated by wildlife artists who study both live birds and museum collections to provide as much detail as possible in each drawing and to capture something of the 'jizz' of each species.

In order to get the best value from your field guide, you need to read it right through, at least once, so that you understand its order and content. Each one is compiled in a slightly different way, with a varying amount of information accompanying the pictures. Some field guides have extra features such as a key to families, a glossary, details of breeding seasons, migratory habits or conservation status, and may contain a number of extra line drawings. All are intended to help you in your quest for knowledge about birds.

The components that are universal to good modern guides, however, are painted bird illustrations, scientific and common names, field notes and distribution maps.

A good field guide will present birds in such a way that they draw your attention to the basic appearance and typical identifying characteristics of any group. If there are several illustrations of one species, you can be sure that the differences between males and females, or juveniles and adults, are important for field identification. Birds that are frequently seen flying, soaring or hovering in the air are most often seen from beneath, so paintings of underwing patterns are useful for the birdwatcher.

Your notebook

The only other book you need to carry in the field is a notebook. Take notes: relying on memory always results in eventual loss of information. We use a cheap notebook for real field work. We also use BOCA's *Little Blue Bird List* for speedy recording of birds seen on a trip. This is a pocket-sized checklist with twelve columns.

Field notebooks need to be of manageable size. They should be sufficiently solid to resist a light shower of rain, or wrapped in plastic if you are going boating or swamp-wading, or expecting a monsoon. Permanent marking pens or pencils are best. Never use felt-tipped pens and preferably don't carry ballpoints; fluids and humidity cause the inks to run and smear.

Day pack or small knapsack

Birdwatchers should carry a day pack or small knapsack containing: a binocular-case (of course your binoculars will be around your neck), a notebook and a pen or pencil, a field guide, lunch, a drink and a small first-aid kit. A local map can be useful.

Some people will wish to carry a camera, a small tape-recorder, birdsong tapes, or a laptop computer. You may need a waterproof torch, a spare set of batteries and an extra globe. Any electrically driven equipment you carry will require a spare battery.

If setting out with the intention of watching at one location for a long period you may want to take a folding chair or stool. Some birdwatchers combine an umbrella with a built-in shooting stick. You can be under it, sit on it, or poke things with it— very useful.

Clothing

Obviously you must dress according to the season, but you must also take precautions against extremes. Don't go to the Alps in a T-shirt, even in mid-summer. Put some heavy garments into the day pack. Aim to keep yourself at a comfortable working temperature inside your clothing, regardless of weather conditions.

Choose comfortable, well-fitting clothes with plenty of strong pockets. Try to avoid needless bright colours, which readily disturb birds (and possibly other people), but a concealed colour patch or bright garment tucked away in your pack is a good idea if you are walking in hazardous conditions. You may sometimes *need* to be seen. Deer-hunting has led to a few fatal accidents in the Americas; if birdwatching in New Zealand, make sure that you know where the hunters are and that you use your coloured patch to tell them where *you* are. Liaising with park rangers before setting out is a good idea.

Never wear clothes that will flap in the wind or brush noisily against your legs, your knapsack or the bushes. Smooth, tightly woven materials are the most practical, as loose weaves can be snagged by branches and will pick up burrs and prickles.

Get comfortable supportive footwear, for safety amongst rocks and in wet patches. Shoes should ideally be soft-soled for quiet walking. Hiking boots are probably best for any but the shortest distances. They offer some support and also protect your ankles and lower legs against sharp vegetation, snakes, ants and leeches. Thongs and open-toed sandals are not recommended for rough walking conditions (and may nullify your insurance cover if worn on group excursions). They may be useful for a camp shower, but little else.

In the middle of the day in hot weather, many birds sensibly seek the shade. If you are unwilling to copy their example, sun-screen, a broad-brimmed hat and covered arms and legs are recommended. Remember that wind can do as much damage to your skin as sunshine, and even in cooler weather you need to cover up at midday.

Extra clothing is desirable for night-time excursions, especially if the temperature is expected to fall. Always take spare clothes for a trip planned for more than one day. Weather changes can be dramatic and unexpected. And put a sleeping-bag in the boot.

Planning your trip

Before setting out on any birdwatching trip outside a built-up area, you need to do some planning. Planning your journey is half the pleasure. Of course you will research the birds you hope to see. But also, before you set out on a trip, be it for a day or six months, you need to assess the hazards you might face, and take precautions against as many of these as possible. If you are travelling to remote areas, plan to be as self-sufficient as you can.

Your vehicle will make or break your trip. Don't forget to top up the oil, the petrol and the water, buy good security locks, take a spare set of keys, and don't leave valuables in an unattended vehicle. Extra insurance may be wise.

Increasingly, national parks and similar places require everybody to take their rubbish home for correct disposal. In more remote places, this *may* include personal waste. (Toilets are still available in most localities, but hiking parties are being asked to carry extremely reliable plastic bags or other containers to remove their own faecal matter.) Littering is forbidden. So take home all garbage, all food scraps (especially introduced plant pieces), cans and tins, bottles, papers, foils, and so on. Burning, bashing and burying cans is now frowned upon. Some animals (pigs, foxes, dingoes, goannas) will simply dig them up again. As a public duty towards animal safety *please* also gather up any nylon fishing line you discover lying about.

Never camp in riverbeds or creek beds. Make sure you are clearly above the high-water level of any major stream in any part of Australia or New Zealand. Flash floods, by their very nature, happen at the most unlikely times.

In the tropics, watch out for crocodiles. Never swim, linger, camp or sit right beside a tropical stream or billabong in any region within a coastal drainage system. For the same reason, never camp on a tropical beach.

Never camp beneath a steep slope. Avalanches, landslips and mud slides can occur without warning. Be vigilant on New Zealand's volcanic plateau.

Nankeen Kestrel perched on a lighthouse window ledge.
Griffith Island lighthouse, western Victoria

Don't camp, park a vehicle or even have lunch under *large* trees. Branches can fall without warning. Get out of the forest and into the open the moment you feel that you are in the remotest danger. Ensure that your vehicle and campsite are nowhere near any branch or tree that has even the remotest chance of falling. In Red Gum forests in inland Australia, large branches can break and fall without warning at any time—even in hot, calm weather—and each one has the weight equivalent of several railway sleepers. Keep your eyes open and don't take any risks.

Don't light fires in the wrong place. All the rules of general fire safety and responsibility rest on birdwatchers, too. Remember that every piece of fallen timber you burn might have supplied food or shelter for wild creatures.

Declaring your whereabouts

Always tell someone responsible where you plan to go, when you will get there and when you plan to return to the start point. Stick to the declared plan and timetable as best you can. If in cave or mining country, always leave something bright or some identification securely anchored on the surface if you happen to enter a hole by choice. Remove it when you come out.

Dogs and other pets

Do not take your dog or any other domestic animal with you if you know you are going to national parks or any kind of protected forest or reserve. Your pet may be perfectly well-behaved and absolutely under control at all times, but a zealous park ranger may be fully entitled to remove or even destroy the animal. If it escapes from your vehicle and gets lost you'll get no sympathy from us. There are enough feral dogs and cats out there already, without adding to the number.

Birdwatching techniques

Choosing a vantage point

In tall forest and jungle, arching backs and necks can be severely strained from craning upward for long periods. For your own comfort, when birdwatching, look for places where you can stand on the elevated edge of a country road above a gully, on a low cliff or headland above the beach and seashore below, or in a clearing on a hillside that permits a long view over the trees. Then look for birds at eye level and below. Birds viewed from above are interesting. You'll get a nice new perspective as they move about below you.

Scanning the landscape

It is important to look at an area of habitat in 'pieces'. Try to identify and visually absorb every aspect of the landscape. Look for 'sections' or 'zones'. Be systematic in scanning each layer in turn.

Look at the ground in front of you, search the undergrowth, the bushes, the larger trunks, the bigger branches, then the mass of upper branches and finally the canopy of leaves and flowers or fruit. Check the sky all around. Turn to the shoreline. Begin again. Search the beach, then the waterline itself, the far bank, the surface of the sea, the horizon line, the sky above once more. Then turn one hundred and eighty degrees and do it all again. And keep doing that all day long. In time you will learn to dissect the landscape into its minor components or mini-habitats.

Practise this every time you go out birdwatching, and after a while you will anticipate what each portion of each habitat might contain in the way of bird life. A sweeping look at a stretch of countryside gives you its general type, and your eye is instantly drawn to the unusual—a burned patch, a gap where a tree has fallen, weeds, a dead tree, an area of dieback, one exotic tree amongst thousands of indigenous trees. And finding the birds will be easier.

Stalking techniques

Birdwatching is a kind of hunting, except that our 'prey' must never be harmed. As always, the first rule is not to do anything that disturbs the birds.

When you arrive at your destination, the sound of car doors being snapped shut, followed by the boot falling with a bang, will rapidly put any nearby birds to flight. Move softly, talk quietly. Please make no sudden movements such as a sharp swing of binoculars or vigorous pointing. Stop your white notebook pages from flapping. No shouts of 'There it is!' or 'Come over here!'

We repeat: wear clothing that is quiet in colour as well as sound. In the peace of an early morning, when a group is stalking a lyrebird in a forest, the rustle of nylon wet-weather gear is as disruptive as a brass band.

Remember that birds are visually acute. Watch your bird and try to move only when it is looking the other way. Keep your hands still—perhaps holding your binoculars at chest level. Stand or sit still until bush birds virtually forget you are there. Be patient. Water birds can be more wary and may have to be stalked. Most birdwatching is *not* a speedy sport.

Once you suspect you are close to a bird you want to see, and especially if you want to settle down to watch it for while, your movements should be gradual, slow, smooth and reassuring to the bird. Birds are clever creatures. Many species recognise the signs of threatening behaviour and can separate them from the non-threatening. Some birds will desert eggs or young at the slightest disturbance near their nest. This is not neurotic behaviour on their part; it is a defence against predation.

Please resist *all* temptation to handle eggs or to poke at nests as they are fragile and easily damaged. Furthermore, your scent will attract keen-nosed predators. Perfumes or deodorants on your body, which you may not consider strong-smelling, will attract foxes to nests you have visited. People carry the smells of 'civilisation': petrol, vinyl, cigarettes and spices. Do not smoke in the bush!

Tracking a bird by eye

Frequently a bird will be sighted a long way off. In open country or over a lake or the sea, tracking the bird long enough to identify it is fairly simple. Hold your binoculars steady and follow the flight of the bird, mentally assembling its picture until you have enough detail to work out what it is.

But birds don't always fly in the direction you might wish. Birds flying up to, or passing behind, obstacles such as clumps of trees, a row of buildings, peaks of small hills or the troughs of a series of waves at sea, have to be tracked largely by anticipation.

Having seen the far-off bird, fix your glasses on it and track it as before. If it is repeatedly disappearing for several seconds at a time behind obstacles, you must try to guess where the bird is heading, then to meet it coming out from behind each obstacle as it makes its way across your field of view. In other words, you must anticipate the number of seconds the bird will take to re-emerge, and imagine where it will be if it continues along the same line it was travelling on before it disappeared. Sometimes there is even time to put your glasses down for a moment, thereby giving the muscles of your arms and back a brief rest, to reassess your next observation opportunity.

Attracting birds by means of sound

It is sometimes possible to attract small and medium-sized birds to your viewing range in forest vegetation by making sucking squeaks on the back or the palm of your hand or other soft swishing sounds, or even little tongue clicks. As an alternative, try to mimic the whistles of species whose calls you may know well (Grey Shrike-thrush, Rufous Whistler), or produce some other imitation—the cooing calls of doves, fruit-doves and pigeons come to mind.

Some species never respond to imitation, but those that do include, with varying degrees of reliability, several cuckoos, some owls, the fairy-wrens, emu-wrens, grass-wrens, scrubwrens, gerygones and thornbills, some honeyeaters including the miners, many robins, babblers, whipbirds, various whistlers, shrike-thrushes, monarchs and fantails, butcherbirds, and the occasional catbird or bowerbird. Silvereyes may respond, too.

You can also call birds up from heathland and saltmarsh vegetation, tall crops, rank grasses and reed beds, where Weka, Red-backed Fairy-wren, Clamorous Reed-Warbler, Fernbird, grassbirds and cisticolas would be good examples.

But a caution once more: these techniques can be overdone and should not be used too often in the breeding season. The same rules of restraint apply as for playing back tape-recordings (see page 188). In fact, we would recommend that you make your own sounds rather than using recordings, because these will cause less disturbance to birds. On average, you may get the best results in the breeding season, but this is because many species become more territorial and will investigate strange sounds in their neighbourhood. A hazard for small birds is that you can attract butcherbirds, currawongs and other potential nest robbers and fledgling snatchers to the wrong areas, so please act responsibly.

Sound-making devices

Apart from the human voice, several sound-making devices can attract birds.

The Audubon squeaker is a wooden tube, painted red, with a tight-fitting metal rod inside. You turn the little handle at the top to make various squeaky sounds. It can fit into a fob pocket, small purse or binocular case. Different people swear by them, or reject them, depending on their experience.

Good bird sound imitations can be made by rubbing a damp cork on a piece of smoothed or wave-worn bottle glass. Ensure that you carry this safely, so that it doesn't break and become dangerous.

One device that we have heard about but never seen is a 'duck caller'. Apparently this is a small device which, when blown through, emits a suitably web-footed sound that will attract ducks. This is a tool of duck-shooters but bird watchers should know about it. There may be times when it has application and therefore should be considered as a possible acquisition.

Hides

Anything can be a hide: your house, a caravan, vehicles, bushes, tents. But why would you want to use one? You might use a hide to spend a long time watching an easily disturbed species, or if you are engaged in activity such as photography, when you cannot avoid movement that might disturb your subject.

Small, light, *opaque* tents with telescopic aluminium poles make good hides. Some brands need guy ropes and pegs. If you have the sun behind you, be sure the birds outside cannot see your shadow through the fabric.

You can draw temporary hiding structures together from branches at the site, but when you go, leave the environment as you found it. Around wetlands you may find mias or 'blinds' left by shooters: small piles of sticks and branches to hide behind. Try not to look like a parked Wapiti or Sambur stag, though. Remember those deer hunters in New Zealand!

Dealing with wind

Gusting or sustained strong winds do not help the birdwatcher. To start with, your chance of hearing the birds is impaired by wind in your ears, flapping clothing, and wind-generated noises in the surrounding landscape.

Any steady breeze that blows straight into your eyes is going to be a nuisance after a few minutes, and is very difficult to cope with if it is strong. Unsteadiness on your feet may be a problem, and even if you manage to avoid being blown over, watering eyes will interfere with your ability to focus the binoculars.

If rain or fog is in the wind, misting of the binoculars is almost inevitable. On beaches and in desert dunes sand blasting can accompany strong winds. Sleet, hail and snowflakes will obviously affect vision on land, as will whipped-up sea spray when in ships or boats, or when cliff-top birdwatching on the coast. To combat these problems, wear head gear that is appropriate for the conditions. A cowl attachment to your parka or anorak is the sensible thing to try.

Take several hats. Some kind of balaclava or beanie that can be pulled over your ears on icy cold days will save earache and possible frostbite. Broad-brimmed hats are fine for calm weather, but need to be tied on firmly or changed to a head-hugging job in windy conditions, as wind beating on a broad hat will affect your hearing and your ability to focus binoculars.

Stand out of the wind when you can—against a building, on the lee side of a tree or hedge, behind tall tussocks, in the hollow in a dune system, or in a cabin angle on the deck of a ship. You may *need* to brace yourself against tree, rock, rail or stanchion, just to have a hope of focussing.

If you are in tall forest or under large, old trees, it is better to get out quickly when the big winds blow. In very wet weather, or extremely windy weather, being inside the car is often the best option. In stiff winds the car will rock with every gust. Fully open the windows on the lee side of the vehicle and sit well back in the middle if you can. This way, your binoculars, your field guide, your notebook and you will stay dry. Now you can see at least half of what is going on around you. Some of that driving rain may still drip into the car even on the lee side, so be prepared with an old towel or two in your luggage.

Some days it's really better to stay at home.

A bird-observing hide built on the edge of a wetland.
Town Common, Townsville, Queensland

Birdwatching from the car

It's worth enlarging, here, on the subject of birdwatching from cars, because cars make excellent hides if properly used. A car really does screen the human shape perfectly, provided you don't stick bits of yourself out of the window, or wave and yell.

The essentials are a slow quiet approach to the target area and no revving of the motor. Position the vehicle to get the best view possible, remain rugged up if it is cold, and park in shade if it is hot.

If you wish to leave the car for a better view, make a stealthy exit. Wait for a few moments to accustom any nearby birds to your presence. If the birds are shy, it may be preferable not to leave the car at all.

If you are driving, don't be selfish. Make sure your passengers have a chance to see what you have located. The driver sees what rises from the roadside ahead, or flies across in front of the car. A set of signals needs to be devised so that everyone gets the best chance to see each bird well.

Slow down or blow the horn for any birds you see on the road when driving, and take extra care at night. Go more slowly on winding roads, especially towards dusk. Dusk, and very early morning, are both wonderful times to see 'creatures' (not just birds) along secondary roads and all those myriad minor roads and lanes in the country. It should be a delight to go as slowly as possible, just to see the birds. You need to watch out for the larger marsupials that may be setting off for a night's feeding or going home. Be aware of wandering or travelling stock, also deer. Frogmouths, nightjars, goannas, the occasional snake, frogs . . . all are out there on the roads: do not let them be slaughtered.

Twilight watching

Just before dark, birds of sedentary habits will move towards their usual roosting spots. Species that roost in large groups, such as Galahs and corellas, may choose a favourite tree and gather there well before sunset. Laughing Kookaburras start and end the day by gathering at selected territorial boundaries in order to proclaim their ownership.

Many birds like to drink at the end of the day, and a late afternoon or evening vigil near water will reward you with excellent views of birds that may have spent their day concealed in treetops or heavy vegetation.

Unless you have found the spot yourself (and it may be in your own garden), this is an occasion for prior knowledge or advice from other birdwatchers, as you will need to get into position well before the birds arrive and be prepared to keep very still for an hour or more.

Practical experience recommends that, in warm weather, you cover arms and legs, wear dark clothing and take an adequate supply of mosquito repellent. Except in mid-summer or in the tropics, warm clothing is needed because the temperature can drop suddenly just on dusk, and being immobile you may feel the cold. Moving about to warm up will destroy your chance of seeing the shy species. It is worth spending a little thought on your preparations because the experience of being alone at the water with a shy, wild bird while it quietly goes about its daily routine is something to be treasured.

Remember that, no matter where you sit at dusk, some of the birds will be in silhouette against the fading light.

Night watching

Kiwis, night herons, owls, frogmouths, and nightjars are amongst the nocturnal feeders. Kiwis spend the day in burrows. The rest tend to stand about very quietly in the daytime, either in trees or on the ground. They rely on a combination of stillness and a degree of camouflage to avoid detection. If they make a poor choice of daytime roost the local diurnal birds may mob them and their presence also becomes obvious to the birdwatcher.

Many guides who take groups out at night are skilled in identifying animals by the colour and shape of their 'eye shine' (the way a creature's eyes reflect light at night). Not all birds can be found in this way, and local knowledge is needed.

Australian Owlet-nightjars are nocturnal, with very little reflective eye shine. They roost in tree-hollows by day, and come out at night to feed. They have a little round striped face, seemingly covered in 'fur and whiskers' and lovely round brown eyes in the front of the head. The bird's appearance resembles, and can be readily mistaken for, the face of a friendly and fascinating little furry animal peering from a hollow tree spout or nest box. Owlet-nightjars also have hissing, bubbling calls somewhat resembling those of the marsupial possum group known as gliders. We call this 'possum mimicry'. Perhaps it is a survival strategy for retaining possession of a good hollow.

There are many arguments about the effects spotlighting has on nocturnal birds. Some enthusiasts would argue that, as it is the only way to see them, it is a reasonable thing to do, but there *are* definitely a few important differences between daytime and night-time birdwatching.

The single act of shining a spotlight once on a nocturnal bird (or other creature) is said not to disturb it greatly. But what if a group of twenty people spend an hour or two tramping around in the darkness, shining twenty spotlights in various directions as they enthusiastically 'track down' an owl? They may not directly harm the owl, but most of its prey will have gone into hiding. Or perhaps they manage to locate the owl, and each, in turn, shines a light into its eyes. The equivalent effect on humans would be as though someone turned the lights off every time you picked up your knife and fork to eat a meal. When the lights are turned on again, it takes your eyes a little while to adjust to the brightness.

Always consider your actions in terms of the potential effect on the birds.

Professional birdwatching guides

These days, there is such a variety of different natural history tours available that it is sometimes difficult to know how to choose one.

As a beginner, you may decide that it would be interesting and educational to take a birding trip in the company of an experienced guide. But what sort of guide? And how do you choose amongst them?

The first thing you must decide is what sort of experience you are looking for. Let's return briefly to the four birdwatchers we met in Chapter One.

Wanda does most of her birdwatching in her own neighbourhood because of family responsibilities. She regards her birdwatching as time out on her own, and is not attracted to group walks. Her ideal holiday would be a week at a birdwatching retreat with knowledgeable hosts, a well-stocked library and optional birdwatching trips available if she chooses to join them. She would enjoy the opportunity to discuss birds with her hosts and fellow guests, and would learn a lot without feeling any pressure.

Wanda's ideal guide is someone who is happy to show her the birds and answer her questions without forcing her to chase birds from dawn to dusk.

Susan is a member of a birdwatching group and takes every opportunity to go on excursions. She relies on others in the group for help with identification points. Susan's ideal holiday would be a long-distance birdwatching tour with the friends she has made. She is happy for other people to organise her trip for her, and enjoys chatting about her birdwatching experiences to people who share her hobby.

Susan needs a strong and knowledgeable leader, who chooses interesting habitats and makes sure that all members of the group see each bird identified on their walks. She enjoys tours that include visits to spots of local interest on the way.

Terry the 'twitcher' is constantly travelling around to seek out birds to add to his myriad lists. When he takes a holiday, he is most likely to go in a small party with other enthusiasts, but occasionally he will hire a guide who guarantees sightings of desirable rare species.

Terry appreciates the professional, single-minded guide who sets targets of certain species and does his or her best to find them. He is happy to travel all day, hardly stopping for meal breaks and taking every opportunity to add more and more bird species to the trip list.

Keith, the conservationist who is restoring the natural vegetation to his property, travels with his partner to a wilderness area to hike, camp and enjoy the scenery.

Keith's ideal guide is one who takes his time and knows as much about the local plants and invertebrates as he does about the birds. He would therefore be unlikely to join an organised tour unless it were a natural history tour to study the ecology of a special location.

You can see that our four typical birdwatchers might be very unhappy if they signed up for a tour that didn't suit their needs.

Once you have decided on the type of tour you would enjoy, how do you make sure that you get the most benefit from it? Guides do their best to satisfy their clients, but as they tend to specialise it is worth your while to ask searching questions before you make your bookings. Some tours are so well described that you know what to expect, others are long on lists of bird species and short on accommodation details.

If you are unused to bushwalking, or dread the thought of days of bumping over rough roads in a four-wheel drive, some tours will be unsuitable for you. The essence of a group tour is that all the participants share (enjoy) the activities as a group.

Don't monopolise the tour guide. You may think that he or she is the only one with all the answers, but often there will be other members of the party who can help you if you give them a chance.

A good tour guide will make sure you don't miss a good bird. In a group, it is really bad manners to cross in front of and block the view of others who already have their binoculars focussed.

Not all guides have superhuman powers of recuperation. You may enjoy rising at dawn, others of the party may sit around talking birds late into the night. Although conscientious leaders will do their best to make themselves available when needed, don't automatically expect the leader to accompany you every minute of the time. 'Bone up' on your birds beforehand. Knowing what to expect will add immeasurably to what you see.

Guides are there to teach you. Listen to them. If you disagree with an identification, politely ask why they think it is that species. As a beginner you will learn more if you take good notes, take a deep breath, and wait for the rest of the party to explain the finer points of the bird.

Learning from videos

Birdwatching by video is now very popular and there is no doubt that you can learn from such an experience. Visual images and detailed behaviour sequences can give you unique access to the private lives of birds. Be cautious about the voice-overs, though, and don't believe all you are told. There are times when script and narrator are not up to the same standard as the visual footage, and the facts can be a bit shaky. If in doubt, look up the relevant piece of information in a textbook or two.

Injured birds

Birds suffer a great deal through interference and inappropriate treatment. Darkness and warmth for twenty-four hours will allow the bird to recover from the shock of injury. An obvious broken leg or wing can be referred to a veterinary surgeon, but a local wildlife carer is the best person to advise you on looking after a rescued bird.

Mineral oils on the plumage of birds causes damage from interfering with a few feathers to causing death by drowning or asphyxiation, by poisoning, destructive lung damage, or eventual starvation. Birds most susceptible to oil pollution are those which habitually enter water to feed and travel. Consequently, in the Southern Hemisphere, some waterfowl, grebes, penguins, petrels, albatrosses and their allies, gannets and boobies, the Darter, cormorants and shags, some herons and egrets, the fish-seeking raptors, and some waders, gulls and terns are the most likely to be affected in large numbers.

A roosting mixed group of Northern Hemisphere migratory waders near previously polluted mangroves. Caspian Terns (red bills) are amongst other terns in the foreground. Brisbane River, south-east Queensland

The combination of oily residues with other chemicals, such as occurs near drainage outlets or as industrial seepage, is a hazard that may affect only a small number of birds, but is no less deplorable. If you find oiled birds, please seek urgent veterinary advice.

Man-made environments

We may have given the impression that wild and natural environments are the only places to watch birds, but this is not the case because, thankfully, birds have been able to survive and sometimes prosper in habitats created by urbanisation.

Just as there may be minute remnants of the original vegetation in farmland, so in towns and cities some small patches retain their value as bird habitat. Road and rail reserves, where they have not been slashed and burned too often, can form corridors for wildlife. So can long-established street plantations or large old gardens.

If you are birdwatching in the city, remember to look upwards (not when in the midst of traffic, please). A Peregrine Falcon may be hunting overhead, hoping for a meal of Rock Dove (the common street pigeon). The Peregrine, a bird that nests on cliff faces or amongst rocks, has sometimes been able to adapt to city living, treating skyscrapers as if they were cliffs. Welcome Swallows use the undersides of flights of concrete steps as rocky outcrops, nesting beneath the overhang.

Parks and golf courses, if suitably planted with indigenous trees and shrubs and containing ponds or lakes, may provide some birdwatching, but most people are unaware of birdwatchers' fascination with sewage treatment plants. When well-managed as wetlands, these areas become famous for their ability to attract a wide variety of waterbirds and (in the right season) waders.

Old-style rubbish tips, unfortunately, attract the native scavengers such as ibis, gulls and ravens and the introduced pigeons, sparrows, starlings and mynas. We once surprised a White-bellied Sea-Eagle at a country rubbish tip, and although we cherish the experience as our closest encounter of a sea-eagle kind, we can't condone the use of open dumps. There are so many environmental pollutants involved: leaching of chemicals, wind distribution of plastic and paper, encouragement of rats, mice and feral cats, and the possible dependence of some birds on these dumps.

Near Perth, Western Australia, some years ago, Silver Gulls were seen feeding at rubbish tips then flying to the town water supply to wash themselves, thereby spreading salmonella infection.

Where rubbish is tipped into old quarries containing pools of water, cormorants, pelicans, herons and gulls may feed in the contaminated water. Lakes associated with mining operations may also contain levels of toxic chemicals high enough to kill birds that drink or swim in them.

Any body of water is attractive to birds at some time of the year. The problem for humans is to keep the water clean, for the birds' sake as well as their own.

CHAPTER TWELVE

Keeping records

We hope that by now you are well aware that birdwatching means more than just looking at birds.

Despite an often copious literature, much remains to be discovered about the behaviour and general biology of a great many Australasian bird species. This means that even the 'experts' will have answers to only a proportion of your questions. Ornithology has long been a true science within zoology, but, as in many fields of natural history, ornithology has been built on the collection of observations by enthusiastic amateurs.

Anyone who is prepared to dedicate time and energy to thoughtful recording can make a valuable contribution to knowledge about the birds of our region. One of the unfortunate truths about the hobby of birdwatching is that many of the most experienced observers don't always write down the details of their observations.

Written records

A simple month-by-month count of the birds in a specific location, faithfully recorded for five, ten, twenty years, provides a valuable picture of seasonal and environmental change. As an amateur birdwatcher, one of the greatest contributions you can make is a set of records of this nature. Make it available to researchers or conservationists as the need arises.

Record keeping can be roughly divided into two types: frequency of occurrence (counts), and behaviour descriptions.

BOCA has carried out a quarterly count of waders around the shores of Western Port Bay, in southern Victoria, for more than twenty years. Once each quarter, volunteer birdwatchers visit specific locations around the bay and send in their reports. This long-term study traces the fluctuations of the migratory waders and local species such as the Black Swans that feed on the shores of Western Port. Such a study is an invaluable tool when assessing the ecological health of the Bay.

Birdwatchers who keep dated records of bird sightings through the year soon find that they have established a recurring calendar of events in their area. Your calendar could show patterns of seasonal or altitudinal migration, courtship and nesting behaviour, or the visits of nomadic birds in response to rain or local food supplies. It is helpful to include a few details about the prevailing weather in your calendar. Seasonal movements amongst Australasian birds need to be a continuous study.

Counts

To have long-term value, your records must show date, time, location, the peak number of each species of bird seen in each study period, as much other information as you can reasonably write, and the names of other observers who were with you and can confirm your report. This last is especially important in cases where identification of the species is crucial to the observation.

Occurrence records (bird lists) are therefore valueless without date and location. Lists may record the birds seen every day in certain locations or on special bird-watching trips. They may be regional, national, world or life lists. Many enthusiastic birdwatchers keep a life list (you will read in American literature about 'finding a lifer'—that is, a new bird for the person's life list). Many of these lists are very personal. They acquire historical value only if they refer to very specific locations, include the details we have mentioned above, and are repeated over time. They may then move into the category of 'surveys'.

Behaviour records

It is true that, at first, many of your observations may be of behaviour that is already well documented. When you observe a behaviour that interests you (perhaps territorial aggression between two species), *first* write a very detailed description of what you saw, *then* read up as much as you can about the behaviour itself and the species involved.

You may find that the behaviour is frequently referred to. That's good. You can see how your observation fits into the literature. But don't waste your piece of research. Continue to keep records of every similar occurrence. Look for patterns. Does the behaviour change with time or weather? Is it a behaviour common to several other species as well?

Or perhaps you have seen nothing yet that catches your interest. Why not pick a species, a genus or family of birds you really like, *or* some function such as migration or courtship, read it up and then observe it in the field. Establish a working bibliography, and specialise in some aspect of bird study.

It is a good idea to transcribe your initial field notes into a more permanent record. This could be a notebook or the computer program of your choice. Print out a hard copy annually—not even floppy disks last forever. Buy new floppies and back up everything you have done every four years for safety.

When writing up your field notes you might find it helpful to include sketches in order to record the position of colour patches, body shape, leg length, and so on. Include the light conditions, the distance of the bird from your observation point, and the magnification of your binoculars or telescope. Some people travel with a small tape-recorder and describe the plumage and behaviour of the birds on site.

Photographic records

Photographs can be a potent form of sequential diary. Record a *list* of the shots you take, preferably in a separate catalogue or notebook, with as much detail as possible, and also label your photographs well. As a minimum, *always* write on your photos the place of photography, time of day and date, because in as little as twenty years' time your photographs may be an important historical record of bird populations.

If repeatedly photographing the same scene over a period of time in order to record changes that occur, establish fixed reference points, and always take the picture from this viewpoint. Map, or otherwise identify, the points in your diary, so that (if need be) others can find them again in the future. In this way, your record really is a catalogue of change.

Prints, slides (transparencies) and videotape will not last forever. Try to minimise their decay, no matter what form they may be in, by keeping all of your photographic efforts dry, in an even temperature, and not exposed to light except for short inspections.

Audio records

Some skill and money is required to make an audio record of your birding experiences. Obviously a suitable recorder is essential, with a directional microphone, perhaps a sound dish, wind-reducing socks, and magnetic tapes. This is something of a specialised, but valuable, aspect of birdwatching and one with potential to increase your knowledge rapidly.

Recording bird calls will enable you to hear them again later in order to identify them correctly. Recordings form a valuable record of what you heard in the bush, what season it was, what activity the birds were engaged in at the time of recording, any evidence of difference between juvenile or fledgling, immature or adult bird calls. You may also get variation in the calls (the dialect) of one single species in different parts of the country.

The technical quality of electronic recordings of bird calls is slowly improving, but few are the perfect birdwatching aid. Many provide only one or two calls for each species out of a possible ten or twelve. It is well known that there are regional call differences in species that look uniform across the continents, and, in some birds, there are differences in calls between races (subspecies) as well. These recognisable dialects are not always demonstrated in recordings. But for all their failings, recordings are an excellent supplement to the written descriptions in field guides. They are very useful for training your ear to recognise bird calls and are particularly helpful for night birds and birds of dense vegetation.

Ethical birdwatching demands that none of us should use recorded calls to locate and *disturb* birds. Tour leaders have a major responsibility in this regard.

Rufous, Powerful and Sooty Owls are considered likely to desert a nest site at about the time when the eggs are to be laid, or shortly afterwards, if the birds become

This Double-banded Plover has successfully completed its trans-Tasman autumn migration to southern Australia, and is in typical non-breeding plumage. Piles of drifted seaweed are important food and shelter sources for waders. Cape Otway, western Victoria

upset by apparent intruders into their territory (we can only surmise their feelings, but some evidence shows that this notion is valid). The same three species, and the Peregrine Falcon, can also be very aggressive around their nest site and will defend it by direct physical assault against any intruders, including humans.

It is well known amongst birdwatchers that a world-renowned British photographer, the late Eric Hosking, lost an eye whilst at a large owl's nest in Britain. The authors of arguably the two best-known owl books in Australia, David Fleay and David Hollands, have both been mauled by owls during photography sessions. To attempt to call up owls with tape-recordings, particularly in the breeding season, is neither 'playing the game' nor is it necessarily safe.

But the safety of more than owls is at stake here. Many birds, including the rarer species, will come to tapes, but there is a limit to such interference. We think that the limit has already been reached, as an ever-growing number of environmental consultants, tour operators and private individuals are using tapes to assist in locating the more sought-after species.

Because accessible individuals of the 'rarer species' tend to be those closest to civilisation, most of the pressure is on the same small number of groups or pairs nearly all the time. Do you see the problem? It is a cumulative series of disturbances, sometimes as frequently as several times daily. If something goes wrong with the nearer birds, if they leave or die, then the 'frontier' rolls back further, there is less peaceful habitat available, and the next nearest pair is under pressure.

Specimen collections

Museums hold specimens as records. Be aware that the holding of native birds, birdskins (stuffed birds, eggs, nests or even individual feathers) is illegal. Always inform your state museum or an approved fauna authority if you have found a bird worth keeping for educational or scientific purposes. It is a good idea to ring up as soon as possible, to safeguard yourself. Let them know you have just found, for example, a beach-washed juvenile female Mauve Dodo in good order, and you are going to deliver it to them on Wednesday. In that way you cannot be accused of having birds in your possession illegally.

If the dead bird you find is in excellent condition—freshly dead, still fully feathered, beak undamaged—it may be valuable even if it is a fairly common species. Freeze it immediately, wrapped in absorbent paper and then in plastic. Label it with the date and location where you found it and the cause of death if you know it. If the bird is a rare species it is worth preserving even if badly damaged. Tell your museum. For educational purposes, BOCA holds a licensed collection of bird skins collected in Victoria.

Standard names

The latest scientific names reflect current thinking as far as the absolute identity of a bird is concerned. Latin biological names are a universal language. Scientific names are gazetted by an international committee, and everybody in science uses them until another change is considered desirable, or a new relationship proved and published.

By contrast, English, vernacular or common names are an expression of everyday speech, of regional dialect, of literature, legend and folklore. The list from which we have taken all names used in this book has been recommended and broadly agreed upon, but usage is up to the individual. Many books contain alternative names from the past, and you may have to do a little detective work to find out whether your Little Falcon is someone else's Australian Hobby (it is). If you want your records to be publicly accepted, you are advised to adopt the standard names.

The Stone-curlews, for a period of time, were renamed the Thick-knees. While it may have been a desirable change for taxonomists, most birdwatchers rebelled, and now the birds, who knew nothing about it, are officially named Stone-curlews again.

Conservation

There are many reasons why you should keep good records for yourself, but if you want to be involved in more wide-ranging surveys you will find that most birdwatching groups have ongoing projects that involve record-keeping by their members. These projects are often linked with some aspect of bird conservation.

'Conservation' is a catch-all phrase for an incredible variety of different activities. Some people dedicate their life to caring for the environment. Some others think it's probably a good idea, but they'd rather not get involved. Others again manage to ignore the issue completely. It's a very personal matter.

This book is about birdwatching, not conservation, but we believe that it is impossible to spend time watching wild birds without caring about their future. Through intelligent observation, birdwatchers begin to understand the needs and behaviour of birds and are then less likely to cause them harm through ignorance.

Your bird library

A well-chosen bird book collection can bring an infinite depth and breadth of knowledge to your new hobby.

Your most useful immediate purchases (after this book, of course, which we hope will get you started) should be a good modern field guide appropriate to where you live, and some sort of modern encyclopaedia or dictionary of birds that discusses the birds of the world, their naming, their distribution, and a bit of their biology—which succinctly puts everything into a wider perspective. Everything else you buy is a bonus, a pleasure, a surprise, a delight.

Every natural history subject, ornithology included, has a voluminous literature. The literature of birds is something like an evolutionary tree. There are systematic lists (checklists) at the 'root' of it all, atlases of distribution maps, various bird biology handbooks and manuals, field guides, the 'how to do it' books (this is one), the broader scale 'where to find birds in an area' books, the little local regional guides, the numerous essays on bird photography and art, the literary anthologies and anecdotal books on birds, autobiographies and biographies of ornithologists, the aviculture genre, and peripheral subjects in all directions.

A good-quality world or national atlas is a useful extra. You don't have to pay a fortune. Go to book sales, opportunity shops and second-hand bookshops—and have fun!

PART FIVE:

Support

Yellow-plumed Honeyeater. Tucked safely against a tree trunk, a newly fledged
and 'just flying' Yellow-plumed Honeyeater waits for its next meal to be delivered.
The yellow gape skin and wisps of natal down show how young the bird is.
Mungo National Park, New South Wales

Boardwalk providing visitor access to a bird-rich wetland.
Bool Lagoon, South Australia

Birdwatching societies

Australia

Bird Observers Club of Australia (BOCA)
National Headquarters
183 Springvale Road
Nunawading Victoria 3131
Tel.: 03 9877 5342
Fax: 03 9894 4048

The following can all be contacted through
BOCA:
- Australian Bird Study Association
- Canberra Ornithological Society
- New South Wales Ornithological Society
- Queensland Ornithological Society
- Royal Australasian Ornithologists Union
  (Birds Australia)
- South Australian Ornithological Association
- Victorian Ornithological Research Group
- Western Australian Field Naturalists Club.

New Zealand

Royal Forest & Bird
Protection Society
PO Box 27
194 Upper Willis Street
Wellington
Tel: 04 385 7374
Fax: 04 385 7373

Ornithological Society of
New Zealand
PO Box 316
Drury
South Auckland
  OR
PO Box 12397
Wellington
Tel/Fax: 09 294 8334

Further reading

All books listed are first editions unless otherwise stated. We feel that, for series or long-running titles, it is important to obtain the latest books or the most recent printings available. This book list focuses only on a selection to help the new birdwatcher. No attempt is made here to summarise the numerous specialist books for identifying families, genera or species. To mention even one is to do an injustice to all the rest.

The following list begins with a dictionary and several worldwide lists, and moves on to general Australasian books, then to regions. We recommend that you pursue bird books in all directions. There are some great books about.

World

Campbell, Bruce & Lack, Elizabeth (eds) 1985 *A Dictionary of Birds*. T. & A.D. Poyser, Calton, England. A really useful bird dictionary.

Clements, J.F. 1991 *Birds of the World: A Checklist*. Ibis Publishing Co., Vista, California, USA. Popular list to species level.

Gruson, E.S. 1976 *A Checklist of the Birds of the World*. Collins, London. Popular list to species level.

Howard, R. and Moore, A. 1984 *A Complete Checklist of the Birds of the World*. Macmillan, London. Heavy little book, but useful list of names to subspecies level.

Walters, Michael 1980 *The Complete Birds of the World*. Reed, Sydney. Popular list to species level.

Australia

BOCA publications

The Bird Observers Club of Australia's monthly magazine *The Bird Observer* provides informal notes and easy-to-read articles about Australian native birds.

The club's *The Australian Bird Watcher* is a quarterly journal of field ornithology for the serious student of bird behaviour.

A Field Guide to Australian Birdsong is a pioneering attempt by BOCA to publish the calls and songs of all Australian birds in taxonomic order.

General books and reports

Balmford, R. 1990 *The Beginner's Guide to Australian Birds*. 2nd edn. Penguin, Ringwood. A business-like, wider ranging treatment of the topic than we have chosen to present.

Beruldsen, G. 1980 *A Field Guide to Nests and Eggs of Australian Birds*. Rigby, Adelaide. A guide with coloured photography; the only recent comprehensive nest and egg guide.

Blakers, M., Davies, S.J.J.F. and Reilly, P.N. 1984 *The Atlas of Australian Birds*. Melbourne University Press, Melbourne.

Bransbury, J. 1992 *Where to Find Birds in Australia*. 2nd edn, Waymark Publishing, Fullarton, South Australia.

Campbell, A.J. 1900 (facsimile edn) 1974 *Nests and Eggs of Australian Birds*. Vol. 1, Wren, Melbourne. Fascinating early text.

Cayley, N.W. 1931 *What Bird is That?* Angus &

Robertson, Sydney. The original 'Cayley'.

Cayley, N.W. 1987 *What Bird is That?* Angus & Robertson Publishers, Sydney. Revised by Terence Lindsey.

Christidis, L. and Boles, W.E. 1994 'The taxonomy and species of birds of Australia and its territories'. *Monograph* No. 2, RAOU, Melbourne, 112 pp. The current official checklist of scientific and English names, and the sequential arrangement of the birds.

Elliot, R. 1994 *Attracting Wildlife to Your Garden*. Lothian, Port Melbourne. Excellent text; good diagrams, photos; many universal principles of DIY bird attracting included.

Frith, H.J. (ed.) 1986 *Reader's Digest Complete Book of Australian Birds*, 2nd edn, Reader's Digest Services, Sydney. A photographic anthology.

Garnett, S. (ed.) 1993 *Threatened and Extinct Birds of Australia*. 2nd edn, *R.A.O.U. Report* No. 82, Hawthorn East, Victoria. A neat catalogue of calamity.

Kloot, T. and McCulloch, E.M. 1980 *Birds of Australian Gardens*. Rigby, Adelaide. Large format; excellent text; brilliant paintings by Peter Trusler.

McCulloch, E.M. 1987 *Your Garden Birds*. Hyland House, Melbourne. A homely treatment of the topic.

Macdonald, J.D. 1987 *The Illustrated Dictionary of Australian Birds by Common Name*. Reed, Sydney. Invaluable for bird names in the various books.

Macdonald, J.D. 1992 *Birds of Australia, A Summary of Information*. 4th edn. Reed, Sydney. A satisfyingly fat paperback; illustrated by Peter Slater.

Morcombe, M. 1990 *The Great Australian Bird Finder*, Lansdowne, Melbourne. Where to find birds.

Pizzey, G. 1988 *A Garden of Birds*. Viking, South Yarra, Victoria. A book to read and enjoy; good photographs.

Pizzey, G. 1996 *A Field Guide to the Birds of Australia*. 2nd edn. Angus & Robertson HarperCollins Publishers, Sydney. Just superseded but widely in use; field guide with painted artwork.

Pizzey, G. and Knight, F. 1997 *A Field Guide to the Birds of Australia*. Angus & Robertson HarperCollins Publishers, Sydney. Field guide with painted artwork.

Rowley, I. 1975 *Birdlife*. Collins, Sydney. A fine essay on bird behaviour in Australia.

Simpson, K. and Day, N. 1996 *Field Guide to the Birds of Australia*. 5th edn, Viking, Ringwood.

Field guide with painted artwork.

Simpson, K. and Day, N. 1997 *Simpson & Day's CD Birds of Australia*. CD-ROM, version 4.1. Natural Learning, Sydney. Contains contents of the 5th edn of the *Field Guide to the Birds of Australia*, bird songs of more than 500 species, the Christidis and Boles (1994) checklist, and other features.

Slater, P., Slater, P. and Slater R. 1986 *The Slater Field Guide to Australian Birds*. Rigby, Adelaide. Field guide with painted artwork. Portable, useful in conjunction with Simpson & Day (1996) and Pizzey & Knight (1997).

Thomas, R. and Thomas, S. 1996 *The Complete Guide to Finding the Birds of Australia*. Frogmouth Publications, Cottenham, Cambridge, UK. A summary of birdwatching sites.

Trounson, D. and Trounson M. 1987 *Australia Land of Birds*. Collins Australia, Sydney. An excellent series of small colour photographs shows off virtually all of Australia's birds.

Regional bird lists, guides and reports

Australian Capital Territory

Taylor, McC. and Canberra Ornithologists Group 1992 *Birds of the A.C.T.: An Atlas*. COG, Canberra. Definitive local bird distribution maps.

Taylor, McC. and Day, N. 1993 *Field Guide to the Birds of the ACT*. National Parks Association of the ACT, Woden, ACT. Neat little pocket book; painted illustrations.

New South Wales

Blakers, M. and Corringham, R. 1988 *Birds of the Blue Mountains*. A Three Sisters Publication, Winmallie, NSW. Local booklet; fair text and colour photos.

Cooper, R.M; and McAllan, I.A.W. 1995 *The Birds of Western New South Wales: A Preliminary Atlas*. NSW Bird Atlassers Inc., Albury. Definitive bird distribution maps.

Hutton, Ian 1991 *Birds of Lord Howe Island Past and Present*. The Author, Coffs Harbour, NSW. Good colour photographs.

New South Wales National Parks and Wildlife Service 1995 *Birds of the Iluka Area*, Central Eastern Rainforest Reserves of Australia. NSW National Parks and Wildlife Service. Local booklet.

Rankin, Neil 1989 *Birds of Wolli Creek*. Wolli Creek Preservation Society Inc., Sydney. Local booklet. Wolli Creek is south of Sydney, and north of Botany Bay, NSW

Roberts, Peter 1993 *Birdwatcher's Guide to the Sydney Region.* Kangaroo Press, Kenthurst, NSW. Locality guide with maps and small colour photos.

Smith, Judy and Smith, Peter 1990 *Fauna of the Blue Mountains.* Kangaroo Press, Kenthurst, NSW. Includes birds.

Northern Territory

Goodfellow, Denise 1996 *Birds of Darwin, Mangroves & Mudflats.* The Author, Winnellie, NT. Local booklet; good text; nine plates of coloured sketches.

Thompson, H. and Goodfellow, D. 1987 *Common Birds of the Darwin Area.* Sandpiper Productions, Winnellie, NT. Good local booklet but out of print—see your library.

Queensland

Durrant, B. and MacRae, I. (eds) 1994 *Birds of Bribie Island, Pumicestone Passage and Environs.* Bribie Island Environmental Protection Society Inc., Bribie Island. Good local booklet.

Garnett, S. 1988 *Birds of the Townsville Town Common.* Queensland National Parks and Wildlife Service, Townsville, Australia. 2nd edn; brief texts; painted and drawn artwork.

Nielsen, L. 1991 *Birds of Lamington National Park and Environs.* The Author, Canungra, Queensland. Good local booklet.

Nielsen, L. 1996 *Birds of Queensland's Wet Tropics and Great Barrier Reef and Where to Find Them.* Gerrard Industries, Bowden, South Australia. Field guide with painted artwork; also many locality maps and good bird watching localities listed.

Town Common Natural History Association 1993 *Guide to the Most Common Birds of the Townsville Town Common.* Town Common Natural History Association, Townsville, North Queensland. Good local brochure.

Wieneke, Jo (ed.) 1989 *Birds of Townsville and Where to Find Them.* Wildlife Preservation Society Townsville, and Townsville City Council, Queensland. Good local booklet.

Wieneke, Jo 1992 *Where to Find Birds in North East Queensland.* The Author, Belgian Gardens, Queensland. Local guide book; brief bird texts, good maps and localities.

Wieneke, Jo 1996 *Birds of Magnetic Island.* The Author, Townsville, Queensland. Good local booklet; line drawings.

South Australia

Baxter, C. and Berris, M. 1989 *An Annotated List of the Birds of Kangaroo Island.* National Parks and Wildlife Service, Adelaide. Good local booklet.

Paton, D.C., Carpenter, G. and Sinclair, R.G. 1994 'A Second Bird Atlas of the Adelaide Region. Part 1: Changes in the distribution of birds, 1974–75 vs 1984–85', *South Australian Ornithologist* 31 (7), 151–93. Text to accompany Stove, Kathy 1994—see below.

Stove, Kathie (ed.) 1994 'A Second Bird Atlas of the Adelaide Region. Part 2: Distribution maps 1984–1985', *South Australian Ornithologist* 31 (8), 195–265. Definitive local bird distribution maps; contact the Association for copies.

Tasmania

Green, R.H. 1995 *The Fauna of Tasmania: Birds.* Potoroo Press, Launceston, Tasmania. Recent excellent text; many colour photos.

Victoria

Bould, A., Bould, I. et al 1995 *Raymond Island Flora and Fauna.* Raymond Island Advancement League Inc., Bairnsdale, Victoria. Good very local booklet.

Bridley, A. 1991 *Birds of the Bendigo District.* The Bendigo Field Naturalists Club, Bendigo, Victoria. Authoritative local text.

Chapman, A., Dann, P. and Legge, D. ND (1987) *Anderson's Inlet Waders and Waterbirds.* South Gippsland Conservation Society, Victoria. Very local booklet.

Cooper, R.P. 1975 *Wilson's Promontory National Park and its Avifauna.* BOCA, Melbourne. Older booklet but still the best available.

Emison, W.B., Beardsell, C.M., Norman, F.I. and Loyn, R.H. 1987 *Atlas of Victorian Birds.* Victorian Department of Conservation, Forests and Lands, and RAOU, Melbourne. Definitive bird distribution maps.

Friends of the Maribyrnong Valley Inc. 1987 *Birds of the Maribyrnong Valley.* Friends of the Maribyrnong Valley Inc., Ascot Vale, Victoria. Good local booklet; line drawings.

Garnett, S. *et al* 1986 *Birds of Port Phillip Bay.* Ministry for Planning and Environment, Victoria. Local booklet; distribution maps and tables, good colour photos.

McCann, I.R. 1982 *Grampians Birds, An Illustrated Checklist.* Halls Gap Tourist Information Centre, Halls Gap, Victoria. Very local booklet; colour photos.

Norris, M. (ed.) *et al* 1995 *Local Birds of Bayside.* Bayside City Council, Sandringham, Victoria. Good local booklet; where to find birds; line drawings.

Pascoe, Bruce and Mallacoota School 1979 *Birds of Mallacoota.* Mallacoota School, Victoria. Older but good, very local booklet.

Pescott, Trevor 1983 *Birds of Geelong.* Neptune Press, Newtown, Victoria. Good local book; black and white photography.

Thomas, Roger and Wheeler, Jack 1983 *Birds of the Ballarat Region: A Guide to Identification, Numbers, Dates and Places*. Roger Thomas, Ballarat, Victoria. Authoritative local book.

Warringal Conservation Society 1981 *Birds of Heidelberg and the Yarra Valley*. Warringal Conservation Society, Rosanna, Victoria. Good local booklet; line drawings.

Western Australia

Barrett, G., Chapman, A, and Blythe, M. 1995 *Common Birds of Kalgoorlie-Boulder*. Goldfields Naturalists Club Inc., Kalgoorlie, WA. Local booklet; brief texts, good colour photos.

Collins, Peter 1995 *The Birds of Broome. An Annotated List*. Broome Bird Observatory, Broome, WA. Good local booklet; annotated bird list.

Marr, N. 1986 *Where to Find Birds in Western Australia*. Kangaroo Press, Kenthurst, NSW. Good local booklet; localities, maps, colour photos.

Saunders, D.A. and Ingram, J.A. 1995 *Birds of Southwestern Australia. An Atlas of Changes in Distribution and Abundance of the Wheatbelt Fauna*. Surrey Beatty & Sons, Chipping Norton, NSW, in association with CSIRO Division of Wildlife and Ecology, Western Australian Laboratory. For reference.

Serventy, D.L. and Whittell, H.M. 1962 *Birds of Western Australia*. Paterson Brokensha, Perth, WA. 3rd edn. Early field guide with some coloured artwork.

Storr, G.M. and Johnstone, R.E. 1979 *Field Guide to the Birds of Western Australia*. Western Australian Museum, Perth, WA. Field guide with painted artwork.

Thomas, C. and Graham, G. 1996 *Common Birds of the Kimberley*. Department of Conservation and Land Management, Como, WA. Pocket booklet; brief text, good colour photos.

Thomas, C. and Dell, J. ND (1996) *Common Birds in the Backyard*. Department of Conservation and Land Management, Como, WA. Pocket booklet; brief text, good colour photos.

Thomas, C. ND (1996) *Common Birds of the South-West Forests*. Department of Conservation and Land Management, Como, WA. Pocket booklet; brief text, good colour photos.

Van Delft, R. 1988 *Birding Sites Around Perth*. University of Western Australia Press, Nedlands, WA. Good local booklet; colour photos.

New Caledonia

Hannecart, F. and Letocart, Y. 1980 *Oiseaux de Nlle Calédonie et des Loyautés* Vols 1 and 2 1983 (both). The Authors, Noumea. Photographic anthology; French/English text and captions.

New Guinea

Beehler, B.M. *et al.* 1986 *Birds of New Guinea*. Princeton University Press, USA. A really comprehensive field guide with 48 colour plates.

Coates, B.J. 1985 'The Birds of Papua New Guinea, Including the Bismark Archipelago and Bougainville', Vol. I. Non-Passerines; also Vol. II. Passerines 1990 (both) Dove Publications, Alderly, Queensland. A superb set of photos and excellent text.

New Zealand

General books and reports

Bull, P.C., Gaze, P.D. and Robertson, C.J.R. 1985 *The Atlas of Bird Distribution in New Zealand*. OSNZ, Wellington. Definitive bird maps.

Chambers, S. 1989 *Birds of New Zealand: Locality Guide*. Arun, Hamilton. Very useful; partly a field guide, partly a locality guide. Good colour photos and many maps.

Falla, R.A., Sibson, R.B. and Turbott, E.G. 1979 *The New Guide to the Birds of New Zealand and Outlying Islands*. William Collins, Auckland. Field guide with painted artwork.

Gill, B.J. and Heather, B.D. 1990 *A Flying Start— Commemorating Fifty Years of the Ornithological Society of New Zealand, 1940–1990*. Random Century, Auckland. A wide-ranging summary of NZ ornithology.

Gill, B.J. and Martinson, P. 1991 *New Zealand's Extinct Birds*. Random Century, Auckland. Fascinating treatise on what has been lost.

Heather, Barrie and Robertson, Hugh 1996 *The Field Guide to the Birds of New Zealand*. Illustrated by Derek Onley. Viking, Auckland. Field guide with painted artwork.

McKenzie, Ross 1972 *In Search of Birds in New Zealand, How and where to Find Them*, Reed, Wellington. Lists 46 localities in detail, accompanied by black and white photos and clear maps.

Moon, G. 1992 *A Field Guide to New Zealand Birds*. Reed (Octopus), Auckland. Photographic field guide; fine photos.

Reader's Digest Services 1985 *The Reader's Digest Complete Book of New Zealand Birds.* Sydney. Large format photographic anthology; very useful.

Soper, M.F. 1984 *Birds of New Zealand and Outlying Islands.* Whitcoulls, Christchurch.

Soper, M.F. 1986 *New Zealand Birds.* Whitcoulls Limited, Christchurch. A composite volume based on two prior books, *New Zealand Bird Portraits* (1963) and *More New Zealand Bird Portraits* (1965).

Turbott, E.G. 1990 *Checklist of the Birds of New Zealand and the Ross Dependency, Antarctica.* 3rd edn. Random Century in association with Ornithological Society of New Zealand Inc., Auckland.

Regional bird lists, guides and reports

Butler, D., Gaze, P. and Hawkins, J. 1990 *Birds of the Nelson Region and Where to Find Them, A Guide.* David Butler Associates, Pukerua Bay.

Index

Photographs in bold type

Codes used:

(Ai)	introduced into Australia
(NZ)	occurs naturally in New Zealand
(NZi)	introduced into New Zealand
(Ai&NZi)	introduced into both Australia and New Zealand
(also NZi)	Australian bird introduced into New Zealand
(shared)	occurs naturally in both Australia and New Zealand
(shared/V)	occurs naturally in Australia and New Zealand, but tends to occur as vagrant in NZ
(m)	Maori names for NZ species
(no code)	Australia only

Photographic credits

Peter Rogers:
 cover (front, back & spine), page ii, vi, viii, x, 2, 6, 8, 10, 13, 18, 20, 23, 24, 38, 39 (2), 41, 42, 47 (3), 48, 49, 54, 58, 60, 61, 62 (right), 64, 65, 67, 69, 71, 72, 75, 77 (2), 78, 80, 82, 84, 86, 87, 88, 95, 101, 102, 105, 108, 113, 114, 116, 121 (3), 123, 125, 126, 129 (left), 133 (upper), 134, 137 (upper left; lower), 138, 143, 144, 146, 147, 148, 150, 152, 157, 158, 162, 164, 166, 174, 189, 192, 194

Ken Simpson
 page 5, 25, 28, 29, 30, 34, 89, 91, 128, 131, 133 (lower), 137 (upper right), 155, 168, 169, 179, 184

Simon Rogers
 page 12, 27, 62 (left), 92, 107, 110, 129 (right)

BOCA page 171